Juggling Elephants

Juggling Elephants

An Easier Way to Get Your
Most Important Things Done—
Now!

Jones Loflin & Todd Musig

PORTFOLIO

PORTFOLIO
Published by the Penguin Group
Penguin Group (USA) Inc., 375 Hudson Street,
New York, New York 10014, U.S.A.
Penguin Group (Canada), 90 Eglinton Avenue East, Suite 700,
Toronto, Ontario, Canada M4P 2Y3
(a division of Pearson Penguin Canada Inc.)
Penguin Books Ltd, 80 Strand, London WC2R 0RL, England
Penguin Ireland, 25 St. Stephen's Green, Dublin 2, Ireland
(a division of Penguin Books Ltd)
Penguin Books Australia Ltd, 250 Camberwell Road, Camberwell,
Victoria 3124, Australia
(a division of Pearson Australia Group Pty Ltd)
Penguin Books India Pvt Ltd, 11 Community Centre, Panchsheel Park,
New Delhi – 110 017, India
Penguin Group (NZ), 67 Apollo Drive, Rosedale, North Shore 0745,
Auckland, New Zealand (a division of Pearson New Zealand Ltd.)
Penguin Books (South Africa) (Pty) Ltd, 24 Sturdee Avenue,
Rosebank, Johannesburg 2196, South Africa

Penguin Books Ltd, Registered Offices:
80 Strand, London WC2R 0RL, England

This edition published in 2007 by Portfolio,
a member of Penguin Group (USA) Inc.

10

Copyright © Jones Loflin and Todd Musig, 2005
All rights reserved

Excerpt from *America and Americans* by John Steinbeck. Copyright © John Steinbeck, 1966. Copyright renewed Elaine Steinbeck and Thom Steinbeck, 1994. Used by permission of Viking Penguin, a member of Penguin Group (USA) Inc.

ISBN 978-1-59184-171-5

Printed in the United States of America
Set in ITC Galliard
Designed by Tom Hewitson, adapted for Portfolio edition

Dedicated to our families
and to those who struggle with
getting all the right things done

[T]he circus is change of pace—beauty against our daily ugliness, excitement against our boredom. The lion tamer and the acrobat are brave and clever against our cowardice and clumsiness and the clowns make our selfish tragedy seem funny. Every man and woman and child comes from the circus refreshed and renewed and ready to survive.

—John Steinbeck,
America and Americans

Contents

Before
the Story

Setting Up the Tent

Mark smiled. His division was having another great quarter. While his colleagues thought they could identify the reasons for Mark's achievements, only Mark knew the *real* secret behind both his individual and his team's success.

Mark's many achievements were familiar to most in the organization. On several occasions he had been selected to speak to a group of people or talk one on one with employees who felt overwhelmed or disengaged.

Success was evident in areas of his life outside of work, as well. While he no longer had his schoolboy physique, he was still the picture of health. Friends remarked that he had the energy of someone half his age.

He and Lisa had raised three wonderful children. Jackie was married and working in a large company. Evan was completing his bachelor's degree and would soon be looking for a job. Brian had started his own business after high school. Through it all, he and Lisa remained each other's biggest fan and were closer than ever.

The buzz of the phone interrupted his reflection.

"You have a visitor, Mark," his assistant said.

"Who is it?" he asked.

"It's a surprise."

"Come on, Carol," Mark replied. "Just tell me who it is."

"I am not telling you," Carol quipped, "and that's final. If you want to know who it is, you'll have to come out and see for yourself!"

Half aggravated and half curious, he went to the door and opened it. There stood his daughter Jackie.

"Surprised?" she asked as they hugged.

"That's an understatement!" Mark made a face at Carol, led Jackie into his office, and closed the door.

"Have a seat. This *is* a wonderful surprise. What brings you here?" Mark asked.

"Officially," Jackie began, "I had a meeting here in town this morning, and we finished up a little while ago. Unofficially, I came to see *you*."

Jackie's mood quickly became more serious.

"I am struggling with something, and I need your help."

Mark prepared himself for the worst. He feared it might be related to her marriage, although he had not noticed any red flags. He took a deep breath and hesitantly asked, "So what's going on?"

"Everything!" she blurted out. "I love my job, but I just can't seem to keep up. I thought the other two people in my department would make things easier, but I'm beginning to think they don't care *what* happens to the company.

"Brett is a very supportive husband, but he's busy with his own job. We are almost too accepting of our lack of time together, and that worries me. We just seem to be dividing and conquering all the time, jumping from one thing to another. Sometimes none of it makes sense.

"To complicate things further," Jackie continued, "Brett and I are beginning to talk about starting a family. I don't have a clue how I could be a decent parent with my crazy life!"

"Sounds pretty serious, honey. How are you holding up?" Mark asked.

"I'm getting by," Jackie replied. "I go to work and do the best I can, but I just wish I had a moment for myself now and then."

"So how can I help?" Mark asked.

"I'm not sure you realize it, Dad, but I've watched you more than you will ever know," Jackie answered.

"Beginning my own career and experiencing the struggles of keeping it all together, I often reflect on how you and Mom handle things."

"What do you mean?" Mark asked.

"For instance," Jackie replied, "you and Mom have accomplished so much, yet I hardly ever saw you struggle like I do. I just can't figure out what's wrong with me. Not to mention the mess that I have going on at work. All this stress is causing me to seriously think about looking for another job."

Mark patted Jackie's hand. "First of all," he began, "I know that you have everything it takes to lead a full and rewarding life. I have no doubt that you can succeed in your current position.

"Second, I struggled more than you will ever know with many of the same life challenges. Your mother did, too. Oh, the stories we could tell you. We still have moments of frustration now, but it is easier because of where we are in our careers and our personal lives.

"What made the difference for us was discovering an easy way to focus our time and energy on the things that are most important to us. We learned that it is impossible to do everything. We started using the process at work and later used it in other areas of our lives.

"In fact, I have *you* to thank," Mark added.

"Me?" Jackie replied.

"Yes, when you were about five years old, you helped me get my act together," Mark said.

"How?" Jackie quipped. "And if it's so helpful, why haven't you or Mom shared it with me?"

Mark took a deep breath and said, "Jackie, you and I are a lot alike. There was a time when I thought I had all the answers. When I started feeling overwhelmed at work, I questioned whether I could be successful.

"I discovered that I needed to find a way to get the right things done at the right time," he continued. "I knew that if I didn't, it could affect not only my performance at work, but also my relationship with you and your mom as well as my own personal well-being. It was around that same time that your mom and I took you to the circus and I found the secret."

"The circus?" Jackie said incredulously. "You have got to be kidding. You're going to tell me that the circus will help me with life? No offense, Dad, but I think I'm a little old for clowns and elephants."

Mark smiled. "Let me ask you a question," he said. "When you are frustrated or feel like you can't focus or get things done at work, does it seem like you're trying to juggle elephants?"

Jackie paused for a moment. "I never thought about it that way, but yes," she answered with a weak smile. "That's a pretty good visual for how I feel. It just seems like getting everything done is an impossible task."

"How long can you stay?" Mark asked.

"I have a couple of hours before I need to get back," Jackie answered. "Why?"

Mark stood up and walked behind his desk. He opened a drawer and took out a notebook lying next to a tattered circus program.

"Unfortunately, I have a meeting in a few minutes that I cannot miss. It should take about an hour. I do want to talk with you more about your frustrations.

"While I'm gone, I want you to read something," Mark said. "Over the years, several people have asked me to share my insights. I laughed, because I certainly don't consider myself to be a self-help guru. Some years ago, though, I did turn my thoughts into a story, thinking it might make a unique gift for you.

"When I get back from my meeting, let's talk about what you've read. Who knows, maybe something in it will help you find a light-hearted way to deal with such a serious issue."

"OK, Dad," Jackie said as she took the notebook from him. "I still don't get what this 'secret' might be, but I'll give it a read."

Mark gave Jackie a quick hug and headed off to his meeting. She settled into the chair and began reading the story.

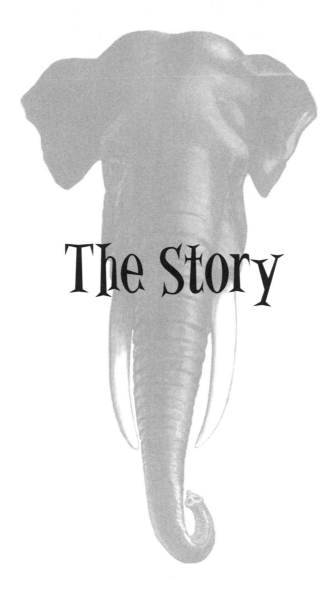

The Story

Tickets, Please!

Mark looked at his to-do list and sighed. His day was filled with meetings, messages, progress reports, and the usual administrative backlog that came with the territory. He knew the rest of his time would be filled with mini-crises and other fires that needed to be put out.

His evening wasn't looking much better. After-work errands and a long list of unfinished to-do items awaited him. "Not exactly a life-changing day," he reflected soberly.

Before tackling his first task, Mark glanced longingly out the office window. He had been relatively successful to this point and was now a manager in a fast-growing organization. At times the workload seemed to grow from demanding to overwhelming, and Mark always felt like his next project needed to be more successful than his last.

Keeping himself and his staff focused, energized, and productive was one of his greatest hurdles, and he knew the challenge would not get any easier with the quickly changing economy.

Normally, he would welcome such challenges, but lately he lacked the mental and physical energy to fully engage his tasks. In fact, his inability to focus on work was becoming a major concern. He wondered how he could expect to accomplish his professional goals if he couldn't work effectively at his current level of responsibility.

Taking a deep breath, he thought about another source of dissatisfaction: his personal life. His new management position required more of his time than he had anticipated, leaving him no time to exercise.

Mark had allowed his work schedule to turn breakfast and lunch into a "grab-and-go" routine of convenience and other fast foods that gave him quick relief from hunger, but did little for his waistline or ability to maintain a consistent energy level.

Having had no downtime in many months, Mark thought about how much he missed getting away from it all. He enjoyed hiking, fishing, and spending time at the beach. These activities brought sanity into his life; the fresh air, simple sounds, and relaxed pace revitalized him.

Mark thought of something else he missed: running. He had been an avid cross-country runner in high school and continued running 5k races in college. His dream was to run a marathon, but career, marriage, and parental demands had eliminated running from his routine. "The only running I do now," he thought, "is chasing Jackie around the house."

Mark glanced at the picture of the two most important people in his life: his wife, Lisa, and their daughter, Jackie. Lisa had always been his greatest source of support, and he was her best friend. Oh, he thought, the things they had been through together. Lisa had worked to support the family while he completed his graduate degree. Mark had spent countless weekends and nights remodeling their home a few years ago. Even now, the smell of fresh paint made him anxious because he knew there were still several home improvement projects on his to-do list.

Jackie, with her big smile and blue eyes, could light up his life like nothing else. The tea parties, "you can't catch me" games, and pretending to be her horse were priceless mental treasures. His smile dropped as he thought of how much he missed those daddy-daughter moments.

Lisa was always good at recognizing when she and Mark needed some time together and was quick to suggest a walk or dinner out. Jackie, however, wasn't always as persistent, and he regretted missed opportunities to spend time with her.

"The circus!" he thought. Mark spun his chair around and looked at the date. In his haste to get his daily plan together, he had neglected one very critical item.

Several weeks earlier, in an attempt to do better in his relationship with Jackie, he had agreed to take the family to the circus. Looking at his packed schedule, he realized it would be almost impossible to leave work early and get to the circus. "Maybe they can take someone else," he thought. Mark immediately called Lisa so she could make other arrangements.

"Not this time!" came Lisa's curt reply. "Jackie has been looking forward to this for weeks; you are not going to abandon her on this one.

"She is five years old and absolutely adores you," Lisa continued. "One day she will be a teenager and may not want anything to do with you if you don't build a relationship with her now. You, Mr. Sunshine, are taking us to the circus today. Be home by three-thirty."

Lisa was right. Time with Jackie was precious and temporary. Hard as it was, he began adjusting his schedule to leave by mid-afternoon.

Arriving home late, Mark ran into the house and called out, "Are you ready to go yet?"

Lisa appeared from the living room. "Late again, huh?"

"Don't start with me," he replied with a roll of his eyes as Jackie ran toward him.

Dressed in red shirt, purple pants, and black shoes, she said, "Daddy, how do I look?"

"Perfect," he said, giving her a warm hug.

Mark thought about changing into some comfortable clothes, but since they were already late, he quickly took Jackie in his arms and they all headed for the circus.

But Where's the Top Hat?

After stepping on several feet while finding their seats in the dark, Mark, Lisa, and Jackie settled in to enjoy what was left of the first half of the circus. The look on Mark's face made it obvious he didn't want to be there.

"At least *try* to act like you're enjoying yourself," Lisa whispered. "Don't ruin Jackie's day, too." He nodded agreement, but still wished he could get back to work.

It wasn't long before Mark recalled why children love the circus. One minute Jackie's eyes were fixed on the tightrope walkers, watching their every move, the next she was laughing at the clowns in their slapstick routines, then she stood to imitate the moves of the dancing bears as her attention moved from ring to ring.

Thoughts about work kept Mark's enthusiasm in check. He wondered about the outcome of the afternoon budget meeting and hoped that Karen finished the weekly report and got it off to the corporate office on time.

A tug on his arm brought him back to reality. All this excitement had led Jackie to one inevitable conclusion: "I'm hungry," she said. While he dreaded the walk back to the lobby, he saw it as an opportunity to check on things at work.

As he stepped into the hallway, Mark looked at his phone to see if anyone had called. There were several messages, one urgent. That one was from his assistant about a proposal that was due next week. The deadline had slipped his mind. He called two members of his staff, but they had gone home for the day. He made a couple of quick notes on the back of his circus ticket to jog his memory later.

He was about to make another phone call when he heard the music rising, signaling that the first half was almost over. He hurried toward the food vendors to beat the intermission rush.

The aroma of hot dogs, peanuts, melted cheese, and popcorn reminded him that *his* favorite part of the circus was the food. It made him want to walk up to the counter and say, "I'll take three of everything!"

A lack of willpower, in fact, was part of his challenge. He would sometimes reason that he could eat certain foods because he would "work them off" at the gym. Unfortunately, he rarely made it to the gym these days because there simply wasn't time for it on his schedule. He ordered hot dogs for Jackie and Lisa and popcorn for himself, then headed back to his seat.

Mark handed the food to the girls and sat down to listen to the rest of his messages. Jackie kept talking about all he had missed. She bounced around the seats with her pent-up energy and excitement. Mark motioned with his free hand to get her to stop so he could hear his messages.

After three unsuccessful attempts to calm her down, Mark looked at Lisa and said, "Can you please deal with her for a minute? I have to make this call." Lisa gave him a "we'll talk later" glance, then struck up a conversation with Jackie about the roustabouts setting up for the next act in one of the rings.

Mark made his phone call, but the person he needed to talk to was unavailable. He sighed in frustration and shook his head. "Of all the days to be at the circus," he thought ruefully.

The man sitting next to Mark said, "Your daughter is a bundle of energy! *She* should be in the circus."

"If you ask me," Mark said, "she's already in one . . . MINE!"

Jackie noticed that Mark was off the phone. "What do you like best about the circus, Daddy?" she asked.

"I don't know," he replied. "The tigers, I guess," he said, making up an answer.

Jackie frowned. "Daddy, I did not see any tigers in the circus."

Sensing the need to lighten the moment, the stranger sitting next to Mark asked Jackie, "What is *your* favorite part of the circus so far?"

"It is the dancing bears," Jackie answered happily. She imitated their movements, stepping on Mark's feet a couple of times until he asked her to stop. Lisa joined the conversation. "Jackie, let's get you to the restroom before the second half starts."

As Jackie and Lisa stepped out into the aisle, Mark asked the stranger, "What's your favorite part of the circus?"

"Well, I enjoy the bears, but I'm actually here to watch the *entire* circus," the stranger replied.

"Really?" Mark said. "Without kids?"

"Let me explain. I'm Victor, the ringmaster with another circus that tours in a different part of the country." Victor extended his hand.

"You're a ringmaster?" Mark asked as he shook his hand.

"Yes, believe it or not. I have my top hat in the car to prove it," Victor answered.

"What are you doing here?" Mark asked.

"Our circus is on a break right now, so I decided to come and watch Dominic's show. I like to see how the other circus conducts its performance."

"What are you doing up here in the cheap seats?" Mark asked. "If I were you, I'd be down front or on the floor where all the action is."

"I hang out down there every now and then, but sometimes I like to see the action from the audience's perspective," Victor explained.

"I've never met a real ringmaster," Mark said. "What a fantastic job, considering all of the experiences you have and the people you get to meet."

When Lisa and Jackie returned, Mark introduced them to Victor. As they sat down for the second half, Victor asked Mark, "So how are *you* enjoying the circus?"

"It's OK, I guess," Mark replied. "Jackie is enjoying it, and that's the main reason I'm here."

"How did you like the performer who was juggling elephants?" asked Victor, trying to keep a straight face.

Mark laughed as he said, "Even *I* know that act didn't happen."

"Well, it may not have been performed here," Victor replied, "but it seems like you are attempting it in your own circus. Maybe I should ask how you are enjoying *your* circus."

Mark glanced at him, puzzled.

"Based on what I've seen so far, I'd say you're trying to juggle elephants," Victor said.

"I hadn't thought of it in those terms before," Mark said, "but yes, that seems like a good description of what I'm doing."

"And how's the plan of 'getting everything done' working for you?" Victor asked.

"It's OK, I guess," Mark said, wondering what Victor was getting at.

"Well, you know you can't juggle elephants," Victor replied. **"The result of juggling elephants is that no one, including you, is thrilled with the performance.** It's impossible to get it all done, so why attempt the impossible?"

While Mark wanted to ignore Victor's comment, he also was intrigued.

"You're right about that," Mark said. "There is so much to get done that I just can't seem to give any one area of my life the attention it deserves. Just when I think I've made progress by getting one elephant in motion, two more drop to the ground.

"I really want to enjoy being here, but I also need to be at work," Mark explained. "If I was at work, I would be thinking about how much I missed spending time with my family at the circus.

"So on second thought, I guess you could say my attempt at juggling elephants is not going very well," Mark concluded. "I really wasn't joking a few minutes ago about my life feeling like a three-ring circus!"

"Great!" Victor replied. "Most people don't see the value in looking at their life in such a way."

The result of
juggling elephants
is that no one,
including you, is
thrilled with the
performance.

"Value?" Mark laughed. "What value could there possibly be in your life being like a circus? I meant it as a negative statement, not a positive one."

Victor smiled. "Let me ask you something. When I introduced myself, you thought it would be great to be a ringmaster. Yet you see equating your life to a circus as a negative?"

Mark grinned sheepishly. "OK, I get your point. What I was trying to say was that my life feels like a three-ring circus. Unlike this circus, however, my life seems chaotic. I wish *my* circus had the organization and entertainment I see in this one."

"Really?" Victor commented. "Interesting."

The lights flashed, signaling that the second half was about to begin.

"Do me a favor in the second half," Victor said. "Observe the ringmaster. Also, look beyond the action in the rings and watch how the acts come and go. I think you will make some interesting observations."

Mark was amused yet curious about Victor's comments.

"What can I possibly learn about my life from watching a circus?" he snickered.

Three Rings to Remember

The second half began with one ring erupting in activity, then another coming alive a few minutes later. As Mark watched, he kept thinking about what Victor had said, especially his "Watch the ringmaster" directive. Mark turned his full attention to the ring.

As the ringmaster finished announcing the acrobats in one ring, Mark watched closely. The ringmaster watched the first few seconds of the performance, then walked to the second ring where the clowns were finishing up their routine.

He spoke to the next group of performers and announced their arrival. Looking over his shoulder to make sure the act was ready, he called the performers into the ring.

The ringmaster
has the greatest
impact on the
success of
the circus.

Finishing his announcement, he quickly moved to the third ring where the trapeze act was ending and led the applause for their performance.

Mark soon realized that it was the ringmaster who kept the three rings connected to one another and who sustained the audience's interest.

It would be so easy to miss a certain act or part of an act in a specific ring, but the ringmaster drew the audience's attention to the right ring at just the right moment so no one would miss any of the action.

Mark turned to Victor and shared his first insight. "OK, I see how the rings are connected. It's the ringmaster, isn't it? He is the link between the rings."

"Yes," Victor replied. "Now let me ask you a question. Who, then, has the biggest role in determining the success of the circus?" Victor asked.

"I guess it would be the ringmaster," Mark replied.

"Exactly," Victor said. **"The ringmaster has the greatest impact on the success of the circus."**

Victor recalled, "When I first started with the circus, I thought certain acts were what made it successful, there are acts that some people like more than others, but once I became a ringmaster, I realized it was how I tied all the acts together that made the biggest difference."

The ringmaster
cannot be in
all three rings
at once.

"That seems like a huge responsibility," Mark said.

"It is," replied Victor, "but it is also extremely rewarding. When I stand at the edge of the rings after the performance and see the people leaving with smiles, I know I have fulfilled my purpose."

"Ever get caught in one ring when you should have been in another?" Mark asked.

"Sure," Victor replied. "In training, I would get so caught up with the act in one ring that I would forget to be ready to work in the next ring! I struggled to find a way to manage my time.

"It was not until Dominic got tired of seeing me moving around like I had been shot out of a cannon that he gave me the best advice I have ever received."

"What was it?" Mark asked.

"The ringmaster cannot be in all three rings at once," replied Victor.

"I have to give my full attention to the ring I am in and, when it's time, I must move to the other ring as quickly as possible."

Mark realized that he was always evaluating his life, by *everything* that was going on. At any given moment, he might be thinking about work, his personal life and his relationships—and things often appeared beyond his control.

Mark turned back to the performance and began to notice that although the circus had much going on in all three rings, the way the acts in each ring came and went was anything but chaotic.

There were always roustabouts ready to take the lion cages or clown cars away. The next act for each ring was just beyond the spotlights, ready to begin at a moment's notice.

Mark thought about what his life would be like if it was as well orchestrated as the circus. In that moment, he chuckled. Victor's comments were making sense again.

Mark reflected on what he had noticed about the movement of the acts in and out of the rings. He wondered what would happen if he focused on just one area of his life like he did with the acts in a single circus ring. Would he see better results?

Mark turned to Victor. "I see your point about how the acts come and go so smoothly in one ring. How do I make that happen in my life?" he asked.

"It consists of two parts," Victor replied. "The first step is to have a plan, much like the program you have in your hand. Most acts follow each other in a well-developed order that is already known to work. The ringmaster simply follows the plan.

"If you really want to make the performance effective, however, the second step is to review the acts before bringing them into the ring," Victor added.

"You mean at rehearsal?" Mark asked.

"No, I mean just before you bring one into the ring," Victor replied.

Sipping his soda, Victor continued. "Remember Murphy's Law? If anything can go wrong, it will? It definitely applies to the circus. A constant stream of people, animals and props must be in position and ready to perform. It is not unusual for something to happen that prevents an act from being brought into the ring at the exact moment it is expected to appear.

"As the ringmaster, you have to know when to change the order or do something else," he continued. "If you aren't sensitive to the changes around you, you can look pretty ridiculous announcing an act that's not ready to go into the ring. **The ringmaster always reviews the next act before bringing it into the ring.**"

"How do you know when to change the order?" Mark asked.

"Simple," Victor replied. "You look to see if the next act is ready. If it is, you bring it into the ring. If there is a minor problem, you tell a joke or sing or something else to fill the time. If the act is still not ready, you move on to the next act that *is* ready.

The ringmaster
always reviews
the next act before
bringing it into
the ring.

Mark had to laugh. His company had recently undertaken a major software change and set a date to begin using the software company-wide. Unfortunately, the tight deadline did not allow enough time to train one or two individuals from every department on how to use the new software. It took weeks to recover from the loss of productivity. "It was definitely not the right time for that act to be performed," Mark thought wryly.

"By the way," Victor said, "have you noticed any connections between the three rings and the areas of your life?"

"I know that work is one ring. I'm just not sure I've figured out the others," Mark replied.

Mark's thoughts were interrupted by a shrill scream. "Daddy, there are the tigers! Remember, that's your favorite part." Mark smiled at Victor, recalling his comment at intermission.

As Jackie turned her attention to the acrobats in the left ring, Mark looked at her and knew he had identified part of the second ring of his life. It was Jackie, but not just Jackie. It was Lisa, his parents, and the other relationships in his life.

In circus terms, he would have to say that he didn't have many acts lined up for this ring. He made some time for Lisa, but they had not had a "date night" in several months.

His relationship with Jackie had changed much in the past year. Mark could not recall the last time he sat on the floor with her for a tea party.

He recalled times in recent memory when Jackie would say, "Watch me, Daddy," and he would respond, "I am," without really looking at her because he was too busy with something else.

Mark also thought of some friends who had been asking him to take a day off for a round of golf or some fishing, but he wouldn't let himself take the time away from work. When he saw his friends later, they would tell of their great golf scores or tell exaggerated tales about who caught the biggest fish. He always told himself that he would take the next opportunity to go with them. Several "next" times had come and gone, and Mark missed the positive energy generated by spending time with his friends.

Professionally, Mark felt like he treated the people he worked with like moving parts in a machine. He regarded annual reviews as "a necessary evil" and at times, his relationships with his coworkers were strained due to his competitive nature.

"If my work or professional life is one ring, I think I found my second ring," Mark said to Victor.

"What is it?" he asked.

"It's my relationships," Mark replied.

"Right again," Victor said. "You can imagine how ineffective this circus would be if there were only acts going on in one ring. **The key to the success of the circus is having quality acts in all three rings.**"

As Mark was reflecting on his new insights, the shout of "Cotton candy, get your cotton candy!" jolted him.

"May I have some, please?" Jackie asked.

"With manners like that," Mark said, "of course you can." He bought two bags, handing one to Jackie and keeping one for himself.

Staring down at the swirled strands of sugar, he shook his head as he began eating it. "This is the last thing I need," he thought.

"Of all the things I take care of in my life, taking care of myself is probably where I do the worst job."

"Aha," he thought. "That's the final ring. My 'self' ring."

Facing this one really hurt. A few years back, when a close friend suffered a heart attack, Mark committed to living a healthier life. He had not followed through on his plan.

He thought about the past week at work when the elevators were not working and he was forced to walk up four flights of stairs to his office. Once there, he was so short of breath that he could hardly talk for the first couple of minutes.

The key to
the success of the
circus is having
quality acts in
all three rings.

Mark also thought of the books stacked on his nightstand—the ones he had intended to read this year but was too mentally exhausted at night to open. The days of coworkers asking him for a recommendation on a good book to read were gone.

Mark realized "self" time had become very limited. He even stopped doing little things like playing fetch with his dog when he got home from work. Those few moments had always helped him transition from his hectic workday and renew his energy for the evening ahead.

Mark leaned over to Victor and said, "If I had the ringmaster's job, I wouldn't have to work out at the gym."

Victor laughed and replied, "There is no question that being the ringmaster is a busy job. At any given moment, you have to ask yourself, 'Which ring should I be in at this moment?' and then, 'Which acts should be in the ring right now?' "

Mark now knew that one of his challenges was that he was not being the ringmaster of *his* own circus. He was just jumping from ring to ring, accepting whatever acts were easiest and most convenient to have in a ring at that moment. He was busy, but he felt like he was not achieving the results that were most important to him.

He realized that while things appeared to be going well in his professional ring, there was nothing going on in his self ring. Eventually, his neglect of his individual needs hurt his performance at work. He was increasingly physically and mentally exhausted and seemed to be sick more often. As the ringmaster of his circus, he should have recognized the problem and made some adjustments.

Mark's analysis would have continued if not for the rising music that signaled the grand finale. The performers marched around the perimeter of the rings, offering a final good-bye to the audience.

Jackie, although exhausted from the day's events, waved to them and said to Mark, "Oh, Daddy, thank you for bringing me to the circus!"

Victor leaned over to Mark and said, "Aren't you glad you moved into your relationship ring today?"

"Yes," Mark said. "With what I have going on at work, I know I won't be able to have this kind of time with her for quite a while."

As Jackie pulled on his sleeve to be carried, Mark reached out to shake Victor's hand.

"Victor, it's been a good evening for *all* of us. When you told me that it would be a positive thing for my life to be like a circus, I thought you were crazy.

"You really know your way around the circus," Mark continued, "and you made some powerful points. In fact, you have me thinking of even more questions about how the circus applies to my life."

"Well, Dominic has been a pretty good teacher," Victor replied. "Who knows what else I will learn from him this week?"

"You're going to be here all week?" Mark asked.

"Yes. Our circus is on a two-week break," Victor explained. "We ought to meet here sometime this week. I'll introduce you to Dominic. He can tackle almost any question you have."

"I'd really enjoy that," Mark replied, "but I don't know how I can fit it into my schedule."

"I understand," Victor replied.

After thinking about it for a second, Mark changed his mind and said, "I might be able to break away at lunch on Friday. Would that work for you?"

"I think so," said Victor. "Noon is fine; the peanuts and hot dogs are on me."

They shook hands, and Mark continued toward the exit.

Programs, Get Your Programs!

At breakfast the next morning, Jackie giggled as Mark hummed a tune from the previous night's circus.

"Boy, I think both of you kids enjoyed the circus," Lisa said.

Mark and Jackie looked at each other with coy smiles and continued eating.

Finishing his last drop of orange juice, Mark stood up, kissed Lisa and Jackie, and said, "I'm off to the next act in *my* circus," which left both of them confused. Mark, however, knew exactly what he was saying.

Once at work, Mark had his assistant clear his schedule for the next hour. He closed his door, sat at his desk, and took out three pieces of paper.

On each one he drew a ring, labeling one "professional," one "self," and one "relationships."

"Today," he mused, "is the day I start becoming the ringmaster of *my* circus, and get my acts together."

As Mark began looking at his three rings, he tried to recall some of the things Victor had said. He jotted a few thoughts down on one of the papers:

☞ *The ringmaster cannot be in all three rings at once.*

☞ *The ringmaster always reviews the next act before bringing it into the ring.*

☞ *The key to the success of the circus is having quality acts in all three rings.*

☞ *I need to figure out which ring should I be in at this moment.*

☞ *I need to decide what acts I should be focusing on right now.*

With those thoughts in mind, Mark placed the papers marked "relationships" and "self" behind the one marked "professional," because there was no question which ring he should be focusing on at the moment. He then listed his current work-related priorities and activities.

Mark remembered the roustabouts working hard between acts to change the stage or props, and he began listing the necessary resources or people he needed to successfully complete each of his "acts."

He suddenly felt overwhelmed. "I couldn't get all of these things done this week if I had thirty-six hours in a day. Here I go trying to juggle elephants again," he thought.

Then he remembered Victor's question: Which acts should be in the ring right now?

Mark knew he would need to order—or line up—his acts to ensure that the most important items got completed first. He reviewed his list again and began numbering the items according to their importance.

He was just about to begin his first task of updating a company policy when he remembered something else Victor had said about reviewing an act before bringing it into the ring.

Mark recognized that while the task of updating a policy was important, there was information he needed from the human resources department that would not be available until next week. Working on that task now would not be wise because he could not complete it in an efficient manner.

Taking another sheet of paper, he created a lineup for next week, scheduling this "act" when the missing information would be available.

The sense of direction Mark felt as he worked through the morning was both exciting and liberating. Although he was interrupted several times by coworkers and unexpected events, having a plan helped him get back on track quickly.

He even found himself adding other acts to the lineup. He knew he would not get to them this week, but at least they would be identified the next time he planned his program and wouldn't be forgotten.

At lunch that day, Mark purchased a sandwich from the company cafeteria and settled back into his office. He laid out the paper with the ring marked "relationships" and mentally reviewed the process he had used for his professional ring:

🐘 *List the acts that should be in the ring.*
🐘 *Review the program (list of acts).*
🐘 *Look for new acts that may need to be brought into the lineup.*
🐘 *Line up the acts.*
🐘 *Determine how to make the existing acts successful.*

While most acts listed in his professional ring focused on tasks or meetings, Mark found himself listing people in his relationship ring. He listed Jackie, Lisa, his parents and Joe, a friend he had been meaning to call.

Looking back over the notes from his conversation with Victor, he saw "Success is having quality acts in all three rings." Mark thought about other people he should bring into his relationship ring.

It was quite clear that he needed to get in touch with his friends to schedule a golf outing. He knew it would be good to catch up with those guys.

Mark thought about his employees. He knew that it had been some time since he had talked one on one with them to discuss their job satisfaction and professional goals. He made a note to personally visit with each of his employees in the next couple of weeks. He also added an item to schedule time to share his goals with his boss and to make him aware of some of his concerns. With this step completed, Mark began to line up his acts.

As for Jackie, he already knew what he needed to do with her. He would get some poster paper on the way home from work and help her draw a picture of something from the circus.

He made a note to call his old friend Dean and set up a time to have lunch together. Mark also made some other notes, including scheduling a time to have the new neighbors over for dinner and to call his friend John who he had not seen at worship services the past two Sundays.

Mark liked the clarity of direction he got from the exercise. He leaned back in his chair for a stretch before moving back into his professional ring.

Appearing in This Ring…

"Is something wrong with your car?" one neighbor asked.

Another shouted, "Do you need a ride?"

Mark had to smile. It had been a long time since he had walked around his block, and the comments from his neighbors affirmed this.

Before going to bed the previous evening, Mark had taken out the third piece of paper marked "self" and looked more closely at the acts listed there.

Aware that very little was happening in that part of his life, Mark committed to doing *something*. Although he knew he needed to do more than walk a few blocks, at least he was bringing some type of act into this ring.

Another important act in his self ring would take place at lunch.

On Wednesdays, Mark and several other managers went to a local restaurant for the pizza buffet. It was so good! Mark knew, however, that if he was ever going to lose his extra thirty pounds, he had to start today, not tomorrow or next week.

Mark chose to order a salad instead of hitting the buffet—the ribbing from his friends was annoying but expected. He simply laughed with them.

After lunch, Mark reviewed a list of training programs his company offered for "professional development." He now recognized that keeping his skills sharp was an important part of developing his "self" but also his "professional" performance.

After arriving home from work, Mark had the usual routine of picking Jackie up from dance class, checking on his parents, and discussing the day's activities with Lisa. These once seemingly trivial events now took on a more significant meaning. Mark knew they were part of his relationship ring—part of what made his life successful by his standards.

Jackie's drawing from the previous evening confirmed his insight. Instead of just drawing an act or two from the circus, Jackie added the audience, including herself, Mark and Lisa grinning from ear to ear.

Mark also changed his bedtime routine. Rather than channel surf until he found something to occupy his mind, he picked up a book from his nightstand, dusted off the cover and read for twenty minutes before turning out the light.

Mark had planned to look at his self ring again on Thursday evening, but things were hectic at work. Two staff members had a disagreement over who was responsible for a mistake, and Mark was getting pressure from his boss about a deadline he had missed.

Challenges at work threw him off his schedule for the rest of the day. He realized that he should not have created a lineup that had so many acts scheduled for "today." He didn't leave any room for interruptions.

Mark went directly to his monthly university alumni meeting after work. Arriving home late, he stopped in Jackie's room, hoping to catch her before she fell asleep. He gave her a kiss and adjusted her covers. Jackie mumbled something and fell fast asleep again.

As he stepped into the bedroom, he was annoyed to find a pile of clean, unfolded clothes on his side of the bed. "What's up with this?" he thought. He wanted to shove the pile over to Lisa's side of the bed and let her deal with it. "After the day I've had, the least she could do is take care of the laundry," he mumbled.

"I heard that" came a response from behind. Lisa had just walked into the room.

"Ever think about how hectic *my* day might have been?" she snapped. "You don't have a monopoly on a busy life, you know."

She and Mark spent the next few minutes griping to each other about why things were not getting done around the house.

Mark was a word away from making a stinging comment when he remembered his earlier thought about working on his relationships. From past events, he knew that if he made the negative comment, it would only make the situation worse.

He looked at Lisa and simply responded, "I'm sorry. I shouldn't have gotten so worked up about it. I know you have been busy getting things in order at school."

"It's OK, Mark," Lisa replied. "We both have been too busy lately. It just seems like we are running in opposite directions all the time. I'm sorry, too."

"Feel like you're trying to juggle elephants?" Mark asked.

"What do you mean by that?" Lisa asked.

"There are so many things trying to consume our time and energy. Don't you sometimes feel like the demands are going to squash you?" Mark responded.

"That's a good way to describe it," agreed Lisa.

Recognizing a chance to work on his relationship ring, Mark asked, "How about we fold these clothes and talk?"

Lisa was shocked, but the chance to get the clothes put away faster got her attention.

"Sure," she said. As they worked, they discussed ways to help each other with their busy schedules. They committed to a weekly planning session to coordinate the family's activities. By understanding the family's calendar of events, it would help minimize the number of surprise conflicts and create a sense of order, which would enable them to work more effectively as a team. With the clothes and their schedules in better order, they turned in for the evening.

The Heart of the Circus

"I just don't want to work here anymore! I found something better. Here's my notice."

Mark could not believe his ears. He had hired Jay two years ago and thought Jay would be with the company for a long time.

He had, in fact, become a key member of Mark's team. Jay's responsibilities matched his strengths and interests, and his compensation package was one of the best in the company for someone in his position.

Mark admired the way Jay was fully engaged in his work. He had noticed a slight decrease in Jay's determination lately, but reasoned that it was probably something minor. Mark wondered why he would just leave.

In the ensuing conversation, the only thing Mark could get out of Jay was that the working relationship he had with several members of the staff had become less than ideal.

Jay saw one as too demanding, while another individual always expected him to "clean up the mess" left by another employee's carelessness.

These situations apparently had drained Jay of much of his creative energy, and he was frustrated that he could not give more attention to his own work and responsibilities.

Following that difficult discussion, Mark welcomed the opportunity to get away from the office for a while. Being around the staff sometimes drained him, and losing Jay meant he would have to start the complex hiring process. He could already feel the uneasiness in his stomach.

Driving to the circus arena, Mark smiled as he thought about using some strategies from the animal trainer to get his staff back in line. Although frustrated, he had to admit that the circus concepts were helpful.

It was now almost automatic for Mark to ask himself, "Which ring should I be in right now?" It helped him focus more in the moment, whether at work or at home, especially when he added the second question, "What act should I be focusing on?"

His challenge, however, was that his rings were too crowded. He could get to the correct ring without much trouble, but lining up the right acts was still difficult.

Since there was no afternoon circus performance, Mark was able to drive through the main gate and ask the security guard where to park. He grabbed his bag and made his way to the main entrance. Victor was waiting for him.

"Acts in your professional ring go overtime today?" Victor asked.

"Not only that," Mark replied, "but I lost one of my best performers today because he couldn't get along with some other people in the circus."

"Sorry to hear that," Victor said as they shook hands. "Still think the circus can teach you something about life?"

"Judge for yourself," Mark said as he pulled out one of his ring sheets.

"Quite impressive," Victor responded as he looked over the pages. "Looks like you're getting the picture."

"I am," replied Mark.

"What are all of these items that are marked out and then written down again?" Victor asked.

"I'm still struggling with how to plan the lineup of my acts," Mark explained. "It's helpful when I ask myself simple questions such as 'Which ring should I be in right now?' and 'What acts should I be focusing on?'

There is no
shortage of acts
for the circus.

"My work life—or professional ring—seems more productive, and I feel more engaged in many of my tasks.

"Acknowledging the presence of a self ring has been good," he continued, "and I'm doing better in my relationship ring.

"The simple answer to your question is: I struggle because I have so much going on in all areas of my life at one time," Mark explained. "Add my staff to the lineup, and *I feel like the circus is running me instead of me running the circus.*"

"Well put, Mark," Victor replied. **"There is no shortage of acts for the circus.** Before you leave today, I want you to talk with Dominic. I had the same discussion with him when I first started as a ringmaster."

Mark and Victor walked into the arena.

"There he is," Victor said, pointing to a tall, dark-haired man standing in the midst of a small group of people. "We'll catch up with him later."

They bought lunch from a vending cart and walked back to the arena.

"Victor, I understand that I have three rings in my life, and I recognize the need to focus on a specific ring. My frustration comes in deciding *which* acts should be in my rings. I'm not sure I'm actually headed toward the performance of a lifetime, you might say."

"To deal with that issue, we need to get to the heart of the circus. Let's go to the floor and get into the rings," Victor said.

They walked down the steps, across the sawdust and into the center ring.

"Look up into the arena," Victor said. "Imagine that it's a typical night at the circus. What would you see?"

"People in the seats," Mark answered.

"Good," Victor said. "And what do all these people have in common?"

"They like peanuts?" Mark joked.

"Very funny," Victor said. "Seriously, what do they all have in common?"

"They want to see a good performance," Mark replied.

"Exactly! And if they don't?" Victor asked.

"They won't come back to see the circus again," Mark surmised.

"How do you think that impacts the way we look at the acts we put in the circus?" Victor asked.

"You have to choose the best ones," Mark replied.

"Correct," Victor responded.

"My performance director and I have no shortage of acts that we could place in the lineup. Not a day goes by that we couldn't add new acts to the circus.

"One reason we don't add them, however, is because they would not contribute to the overall success of the circus.

"The circus exists to entertain audiences of all ages and to be a profitable organization that can continue to operate for years," Victor explained. "To accomplish those goals, we must have quality acts in each ring. It all begins with recognizing that **every act must serve a purpose.**"

Victor continued, "Choosing acts based on your purpose works best when it becomes a habit. It's easy to make a wrong choice based solely on emotion, laziness, convenience, or pressure from others who don't have a good understanding of your purpose. No matter who we are, we can't do it all. That is why it is essential that every act must serve a purpose.

"Make the wrong choice, and you will sometimes bring a bad act into your circus," Victor chuckled. "Then you have the 'dancing lizards' dilemma."

"I can't wait to hear this one," Mark replied with a laugh.

"It was about seven years ago," Victor began, "my first year as a ringmaster. Just after the season started, one of the clowns came to me and wanted to add another act.

Every act must serve a purpose.

"Normally, no new acts are allowed without reviewing them first," he continued. "He promised that this new act would be nothing like I had ever seen. I was busy, so I gave in and waited to see his big surprise.

"When it came time for the clowns to demonstrate their individual gags, this clown opened a box. He sat three lizards on a table, signaled for the music to start, and the lizards moved their heads, seemingly to the beat of the music," Victor recalled with a grin.

"The audience had no idea what he was trying to do. I was embarrassed for both of us," Victor said. "After the performance, I told him I never wanted to see the 'dancing lizards' routine again."

Mark reflected on Victor's comments and realized that he had put some bad acts in his circus over the past year.

"I can see where I have made some incorrect choices in my lineup," Mark said, "but my greatest anxiety doesn't come from choosing between a bad act and a good one, but choosing between two or three *good* ones."

"We have the same challenge in the circus," Victor replied. "That's when I have to remind myself that not all acts belong in my circus. We cannot be all things to all people. Choices have to be made."

"But that's what I'm saying," Mark answered. "How do I choose *which* acts to bring into my ring?"

"As I said earlier, it starts with asking yourself whether it fulfills your purpose for that ring," Victor replied. "With purpose in mind, the next question is, 'Do I have the resources to make the act successful?'"

"I have reviewed some fantastic acts, but we have no room for them in the lineup right now," Victor said.

"Couldn't you just drop one of the existing acts?" Mark asked.

"Sure, that's possible, and we do," Victor responded. "But realize that this decision could have a negative impact on the overall circus. Remember, if we plan our acts correctly, every act serves a purpose."

Victor's words took Mark back to a situation his company experienced a couple of years ago.

A new product was launched at a time when the marketing department was already working at a breakneck pace. Research was not properly done, the marketing plan was ineffectual, and the go-to-market strategy was weak.

The product failed to have an impact in the marketplace because time and resources were just not available to successfully launch it. The product was good, but the timing was bad.

Victor continued. "I also see acts that would be perfect for our circus, but we don't have the physical space for them on our traveling train.

"Last year, we auditioned someone who gets shot out of a cannon. It was the best act like that I have seen in years. The problem was that when we looked at the space he would need to transport that big cannon, we had to say no."

"Do you ever get another chance to bring those acts into the circus?" Mark asked.

"Sometimes," said Victor. "We added one act five years after the first time we reviewed it. We are constantly looking at ways to improve our circus, but sometimes the resources are just not there.

"Circumstances change. Performers retire or leave. The circus may introduce a new theme for the year. Any number of things can change our mind about an act and cause us to use it as long as it fits with our purpose.

"We also believe that only quality acts belong in a circus," Victor added. "Even though a quality act may not be right for our circus, it's a shame for the act not to find a home. We may refer them to Dominic to see if his circus could use them, or we put them in touch with another circus. There are always circuses looking for new and better acts.

"Another part of our strategy involves looking not at individual acts, but at the overall order of those acts in the lineup.

"Line up the acts based on what will create an effective performance. In the end, the audience may not remember a specific act, but they will remember how they felt at the circus."

"I understand now why what goes on in the rings is the heart of the circus," Mark said. "Can we stop for a moment so I can make some notes?"

"Before you write down anything, one last consideration needs to be made," Victor said. "It's a lesson I learned the hard way. In fact, I try to forget the experience, as often as possible, that led to this valuable lesson."

"Let's hear it," Mark replied with a chuckle.

Victor began. "Not long after I began training to be a ringmaster, I started questioning how Dominic had the acts arranged in the circus. I thought we needed to liven things up a little and pick up the pace. Dominic finally let me have my wish one night.

"About a week prior to the performance, Dominic told me to arrange the acts in each ring as I saw best."

"How did it go?" Mark asked.

"It was horrible!" Victor said, with his head in his hands.

"At first, the upbeat pace seemed to be working well. Then came a point where I had scheduled several major acts at the same time. The roustabouts were scrambling to keep everything in place, and the audience got confused because there was so much going on.

"The second half wasn't much better," he continued. "Because I scheduled major acts together, the audience lost interest when there was a lull in the action.

"We made it through the night, but Dominic promised the staff that he would not let me arrange the schedule again until I had more experience.

"And I would never *want* to do it again, either," Victor added. "It seemed like a good idea at the time. It nearly killed me, trying to keep up with the acts and trying to be in all three rings at once. I was physically, mentally and emotionally exhausted."

"How does that experience apply to me?" Mark asked.

"Look at a successful three-ring circus performance," Victor answered. "The circus maintains its effectiveness and efficiency by scheduling major acts at different times.

"It would be almost impossible to have enough staff to have all of the major acts take place at the same time, or even to have them follow each other," Victor explained. "Scheduling the acts at different times enables them to be managed better, and the ringmaster can function at his best, as well."

"OK, Victor," Mark said. "While you recover from recalling your traumatic experience, can I write some of these things down?"

"Sure. Just don't use me as your example of creating a bad performance," Victor joked.

Mark sat down and recorded the key points of their conversation:

- *Not all acts belong in my circus.*
- *All acts need to fulfill my purpose.*
- *I have to have the resources to make my acts successful.*
- *I need to line up my acts based on what will create an effective performance.*
- *I need to maintain my efficiency and effectiveness by scheduling major acts at different times.*

The Performers

As Mark reflected on his notes, he wished his staff could hear Victor's words about lining up the right acts at the right time. He thought back to the previous week. A member of his staff had failed to get an important report to his boss, even after Mark had reminded him several times. When Mark got called into the boss's office, he knew it was not for a positive reason.

Mark was frustrated because he didn't think he should have to constantly remind his employees of what was important and what needed to get done.

The relationship
between the
ringmaster and the
performers affects
the success of
the circus.

He realized his assumption was wrong and made a note to himself to review the steps he had learned from Victor with his staff. He knew this would help them better focus their time and energy on what was important.

"Victor," Mark said, "I'm beginning to realize how much other people can affect my circus. Sometimes my staff doesn't seem to listen to me. I feel like we're communicating on different levels.

"If you could help me solve my employee problems, that would *really* make my circus more memorable," Mark quipped.

"Take this morning, for instance. I had no clue that one of my employees was so unhappy with his job. To make matters worse, he told me about other troubles that may be brewing in my department. If I can't keep my staff engaged in their tasks, how am I supposed to stay focused?"

"I have some ideas, but the expert in this area is Dominic," Victor said. "He was one of my mentors in how to lead others. He always says that **the relationship between the ringmaster and the performers affects the success of the circus.**"

Victor noticed that Dominic was no longer busy, so he motioned for him to join their conversation.

"Well, well, is this the new recruit to clean up after the elephants?" Dominic asked in his booming announcer voice.

Victor smiled. "Afraid not, Dominic. This is Mark. He was at the circus on Monday night, and we began that talk you had with me a few years ago."

"I see," Dominic replied. "And are you still trying to juggle elephants?" he asked Mark.

"Not so much in acts where I'm the only performer," Mark replied. "But trying to lead my staff makes me feel like I am."

"You mean they just don't seem like willing performers in your circus?" Dominic asked insightfully.

"I couldn't have said it better," Mark replied.

"I think I can help with your juggling dilemma, but first we'd better get out of the way.

"Duck!" he yelled. At that moment, a member of the trapeze team sailed overhead.

"It's rehearsal time. Let's move to the seats." They walked to some seats near the center ring.

"Before we get into specifics, Mark, let me tell you a little about my background," Dominic began. "I started out many years ago as a roustabout. It was hard work, but I stuck with it.

"From there, I became an assistant with the animal trainer. I was even a clown for a time. In fact, I think I have spent some time in almost every job the circus has to offer, even cleaning up after the elephants.

"As a result, I have learned that it takes every person doing the right job at the right moment to make the circus successful."

"Go on," Mark said.

"It all begins with the ringmaster," Dominic explained. "The ringmaster must be totally focused on his role. He needs to be intimately familiar with the lineup, know the performers, and be able to keep the circus moving along at the proper pace. The performers look to the ringmaster for leadership and direction. The ringmaster has the greatest influence on the success of the circus."

"Seems like I have heard that somewhere before," Mark said, glancing at Victor.

As Dominic looked out at the rehearsing performers, he said, "What I have found in my years with the circus is that every act holds a lesson in how to work with people more effectively.

"Take this trapeze act, for instance. Many years ago, I filled in for one of the performers while he recovered from the flu. I just held the bar, but I gained many new insights about teamwork.

Every member is
important and has
to be fully engaged
on the right acts
to make the team
successful.

"I learned that every member of the act is important. If just one person doesn't carry out his or her responsibility, the whole team suffers.

"Look at the person on that platform. Do you know what his job is?"

"No," Mark replied.

"His job is to pass the bar to a member of his team as they swing from the other side," Dominic said.

"That doesn't seem so difficult," Mark replied.

"Oh really?" Dominic commented. "What if that person said, 'I'm not the star; no one notices me in the dark.' Based on their lack of enthusiasm, they get sloppy and swing the bar at the wrong time, and the performer misses it. What would happen?"

Mark realized how he had underestimated the person's value. "The performer would fall," he said.

"Exactly," Dominic replied with a nod.

"Remember that **every member is important and has to be fully engaged on the right acts to make the team successful.** That's true whether the team is a department, organization, or family."

They turned their attention to the commotion in the left ring, where the animal trainer was working with one of his assistants on getting a tiger to jump from one platform to another.

"John is so patient with his animals. Good thing he's just as patient with his assistant," Dominic observed.

"What do you mean?" asked Mark.

"Well, his assistant thinks being an animal trainer is all about showing the animals who's boss," explained Dominic.

"Cracking the whip, so to speak, is necessary, because if someone doesn't establish expectations and remind the animals of the consequences of misbehavior, the act would be unsafe and ultimately a failure.

"Mark, please understand that I am not saying people are animals, but over the years I have seen many performers come and go. With each new performer or group, we clearly explain expectations and the consequences of failing to meet those expectations. I guess you could call that cracking the whip.

"Some performers rise to those expectations immediately," Dominic said. "Others need reminders about the expectations, and still others seem to be oblivious to everything we tell them.

"It would be easy to just dismiss all those who don't comply immediately with expectations we set for them.

"Just like it would be easy to get rid of a tiger that doesn't learn to perform on command as quickly as the others.

"However, an effective animal trainer recognizes that discipline is a small part of the training process. Getting to know the animal is much more important. Once he understands the animal, he can work *with* the animal's personality instead of always trying to force the desired behavior.

"It's the same with people. Once you get to know an individual, you can better understand how to fully engage their energies to accomplish a specific goal or task."

Mark thought immediately of Jay. He recalled his initial interview with him, in which Jay had spelled out so clearly what motivated him. Mark had been too busy to recognize that Jay was not being challenged in a way that continued to motivate him. Mark realized that his failure to notice the warning signs was now costing him one of his most promising employees.

Dominic continued. "Watching the animal trainer also showed me the need to **constantly offer positive reinforcement for good behavior, and consistently give constructive feedback for negative behavior.** A lack of reinforcement or feedback can create a lack of desire to succeed or even to meet basic expectations."

Constantly offer
positive reinforcement
for good behavior,
and consistently give
constructive feedback
for negative behavior.

Mark thought about a manager he had in a previous company who never appeared unless something was wrong. His lack of praise for Mark's work was a key reason he left the company. He just did not feel appreciated.

"What have we here?" called a voice. "A couple of people trying to watch the circus for free?"

Dominic laughed. "Yeah, and the show's not bad if they just had a better ringmaster."

"Mark, this is April, our general manager."

"Pleased to meet you, Mark," she said. "I apologize for interrupting your meeting, but I wanted to let you know, Dominic, that Sergei just found out that his mother's condition has worsened. I have arranged his travel home and I also thought I would send flowers on behalf of all of us. I just wanted you to know."

"Of course," Dominic said. "Thanks for your attention to detail."

"No problem," April replied. "That's my job. Now if you will excuse me, I need to check on a few other members of our group. Have fun at the circus, Mark."

April jogged up the steps, and the threesome turned their attention back to the circus.

"And I guess you had that job at one time, too?" Mark said jokingly.

"Not in a large circus like this one," Dominic replied, "but I have had that responsibility."

"But her job doesn't seem to be about the circus," Mark said.

"April may not seem like an act in terms of a trapeze troupe or animal trainer, but her role is vital to our success as a circus.

"You see, we have high expectations of our people. They work long hours, travel extensively, and rarely get a break. Some travel with their families; others are here alone.

"People could feel pretty insignificant in this crazy environment. It's April's job to make sure they have what they need to be happy, productive members of the team."

"So April's job is to help fix their problems?"

"It goes far beyond that," Dominic replied. "See that clown with green hair? That's Bruce. A few weeks ago, he was working in a concession stand. Staff members began complaining about his poor attitude. He was rude to customers and just didn't seem to care.

"The staff almost had everyone convinced that management needed to get rid of him. The concessions manager alerted April to the situation and said, 'See if you can find out what's going on with him.'

"April put the pieces together and discovered that Bruce was bored working in concessions. She arranged an audition with the clown troupe, and now look at him. The audience loves him! He's back to being his best again.

"Just think, we nearly lost a great member of our staff because we didn't pay attention to his real needs. The work of the general manager helped me understand that **people have needs that extend way beyond the obvious ones.** April is an indispensable member of this organization."

"Wow," Mark exclaimed, "I wish my company had the money to hire someone for that type of position. We could call that person 'Chief Morale Officer.' "

Dominic chuckled and said, "Yes, that would be an effective title, but don't think that meeting the needs of others should be the job of just one person or limited to a formal position. *All* of us have the opportunity to focus on the needs of others, whether they're colleagues, family members, or neighbors. Whether we do or not depends on how much we value their contribution."

Mark looked at Dominic and said, "Speaking of clowns, I'm wondering if your next suggestion will be that I put on the red nose and pull some ridiculous stunts."

People have
needs that extend
way beyond the
obvious ones.

"I don't suggest that you do the pie-in-the-face routine, but think about what clowns do for the circus," Dominic replied. "They make people laugh and distract them from circumstances around them."

Victor jumped in. "I'll give you an example from Monday night. Do you remember what your daughter was doing when the bears were in the ring dancing?"

"Yes, she was standing up and dancing like them," Mark said.

"And what were you doing?" Victor asked.

"I was watching her," Mark replied.

"What if, just for a moment, you had stood up and danced with her?" Victor asked.

"My wife never would have spoken to me again," Mark said with a laugh. "No, seriously, Jackie would have loved it."

"Exactly," came Victor's reply. "Being a clown isn't necessarily about elaborate performances or gags. Clowns teach us that **people sometimes need to laugh, relax, and not take themselves so seriously.**"

Mark thought back to a particularly stressful time at work a few months earlier. In the midst of an intense project, a department manager stopped by and asked about playing basketball.

People sometimes
need to laugh,
relax, and not
take themselves
so seriously.

When Mark told him he didn't have a change of clothes, the manager pulled three foam basketballs from his bag and placed a hoop from the bag on the door. After five minutes of slam dunks and three-pointers, Mark was ready to go back to work. It was a simple mental boost during a tough time.

"Speaking of acts, I've got one scheduled in my professional ring in an hour," Mark said. "I better go complete my review before it starts."

Mark stood up, shook Dominic's hand, and said, "You have been an enormous help, Dominic."

"There's much more we could talk about, Mark, but I have a hunch you'll pick it up on your own," Dominic said. "Who knows, maybe you'll get the chance to help someone else stop trying to juggle elephants."

"I'll walk out with you," Victor chimed in.

"Victor, I really appreciate your time and insight," Mark said as they approached the gate. "Dominic's comments are very timely as well."

"Be sure that you make the connection between Dominic's comments and your initial concern of how to 'get it all done,' " said Victor. "If you place all the pressure on yourself to get results, it really does feel like you're juggling elephants. We have a phrase we use around the circus that goes 'Delegate or die.' We know that the only way the circus can be successful is if we all shoulder the load together.

"An important part of being successful in business and in life is to have a good team around you, individuals to whom you can delegate more responsibility or who will work harder when circumstances call for it. It's an important way to achieve better results.

"Having a healthy support system around you will strengthen you personally and reduce the number of times you feel like your circus is out of control. I hope you can see why taking care of those teams and keeping them focused is critical, whether at work or in your more intimate relationships."

"I never dreamed I could learn so much from something as simple as a circus," said Mark. "Here's my business card. Please let me know if there is ever anything I can do for you."

Victor smiled. "Thanks. Maybe our circuses will cross again in the future."

They shook hands, and Mark headed for his car.

Dress Rehearsal

everal months passed, but the impact of Victor and Dominic's words and his own experience were permanently etched in Mark's mind and in his behaviors. He now always asked two questions before putting an act into one of his rings:

Does this act belong in my circus?

When should this act appear?

Mark had begun regular performances in his self ring, exercising three to four times a week. He had started running again, preparing for a 5k run that would take place in a few months. He had begun to lose weight and seemed to have more energy for his work and his personal tasks.

Reading became part of his regular routine. In reviewing his "program" each day, he saw that he sometimes had twenty to thirty minutes of free time after lunch, and he filled the time reading a book or the newspaper before jumping back into his work. He found himself much more focused for his afternoon tasks, both mentally and physically.

Sitting on the porch one evening enjoying their planning time, Lisa asked, "What's this I hear about a daddy-daughter date?"

Mark smiled and said, "I see Jackie is no good at keeping a secret."

"Well, I would give her a pass this time," Lisa replied. "She was so excited about it, she was about to explode."

"With my new project at work, I am going to have to spend extra hours at the office," Mark said. "I will miss a few nights of bedtime stories and evening dance practices so I wanted to give Jackie and me something to look forward to over the next couple of weeks. It will help me stay focused at work, too."

"Sounds great, Mr. Popularity," Lisa said, "but what am I supposed to do while you two are gone?"

"Let me see," Mark said. "If I remember correctly, a certain someone said it would be great to have an evening at home alone. Maybe you can use the time to be in your self ring."

"I would like the time to just relax," Lisa confided, "but what is this about a 'self ring'?"

"Well, if you don't line up the right acts for your self ring, your whole circus may suffer," Mark replied with a smirk.

Lisa looked at him like he was from another planet.

"What are you talking about?" she quipped.

Mark went into the house, retrieved his papers with the three circles for the current week, and returned to the porch.

He laid the papers on the table and began to explain the concept of the three rings and the other insights he had gained from Dominic, Victor, and his experience at the circus.

"What I have been trying to do over the past few months," Mark said, "is take time each week to look at what should be happening in each ring of my life and then line up the acts needed to, well, create a better performance. Ultimately, I have come to realize that the effort to get it all done doesn't make sense. Call me nuts, but it's working."

Lisa sat silent for a few moments, taking in what Mark said.

"I don't think you're nuts," she said. "My immediate thought was about something that happened last Thursday. I was at school and my planning period had just begun. I had papers to grade, a class project to outline, and several other things I wanted to get done.

"Instead of working on them, I thought I would take a minute and call our travel agent Tom to request information about the cruise we're planning for next summer.

"When I called, Tom obviously wasn't busy, so he started outlining our options. It was exciting, and I enjoyed hearing the possibilities.

"Before I realized it, my planning time was over, and I hadn't gotten anything done.

"One thing led to another. I wasn't ready for my next class so things didn't go very smoothly. I also found myself distracted because I was frustrated with myself.

"When we had our grade-level meeting after school, I wasn't as prepared as I should have been. And at home that night, I had to stay up late to finish grading papers, which cut into our time to talk. Just that one hour had a domino effect in derailing my whole day.

"To top it all off, I didn't get my regular night's sleep, which made me a little cranky the next day."

"A little?" Mark said with a laugh.

"Careful," Lisa replied, smiling. "Using the idea you just talked about, I could have stopped myself before making the call and said, 'Which ring should I be in right now?'

"Then I could have focused more effectively on getting the right acts, as you call them, done," Lisa continued. "By doing so, I would have had a much more productive day and enjoyable evening.

"Talking about this has helped me realize how much I have neglected my self ring, too. Just look at that flower bed. Five years ago, I would have been out there weeding and planting. I love watching things grow.

"I think that while you and Jackie are, as you say, 'working on your relationship ring,' I'll jump into my self ring and work on those flower beds."

Preparing to retire for the evening, Lisa said to Mark, "I really like the simple concept of choosing which ring to be in and working in that ring."

"I do, too," Mark said wistfully. Lisa sensed there was something more to his comment.

"But what?" she asked.

"Well, Victor said something that I still don't quite understand. He said that major acts should be scheduled at different times in the circus. He said it was about making sure you didn't spread yourself too thin. I still don't fully get what he was trying to say."

"I think I do," Lisa said. "Think back about four years ago. Jackie was one, we decided to remodel the house, and you had taken on a new assignment at work. You were not a happy camper."

"I'll say," Mark replied. "I remember being at work trying to concentrate, but it was hard because I had been up so late working on the house. Time with Jackie was also pretty limited."

"If you were in that situation again, what do you think you would do differently?" Lisa asked.

"That's easy," Mark said. "I would put off the remodeling project for a few months."

"There's your application," Lisa said. "I remember seeing you so mentally, emotionally and physically drained all the time. If we had put off remodeling until things were less hectic, it would have helped you be more effective in your professional ring *and* in your relationship ring.

"Now, if you will excuse me, I need to bring the act called 'A Good Night's Sleep' into my self ring."

Mark laughed as they walked into the house together.

Crowded Lineup

With the new project under way, Mark needed his newfound wisdom like never before. The assignment was more complex than he initially thought. Even with prior planning, Mark could see that his staff was losing ground, and they were in jeopardy of not meeting the deadline.

At the next staff meeting, Mark shared his concern about their lack of productivity. He asked each staff member to give an update on their work and what they were focusing on for the benefit of everyone on the team. As the individuals shared their updates, Mark wrote them on a whiteboard.

He first started with removing any areas of duplication of effort. Then he asked the team if there were any items that could be removed from the list that were not important. Lastly, he asked, "As you look at the board, do you see any areas you could work on together to help each other?" As group members offered their thoughts, Mark wrote the additional comments on the board.

"Now I want you to set a time to meet with the people you will be working with on your tasks, so we can speed up the completion of this project."

The first few days produced no measurable results. Mark was beginning to think he had not handled the situation effectively. A week later, however, Ben walked into his office and handed him a part of the plan that was not due for another five days.

"Wow!" Mark responded. "How did this happen?"

Ben smiled and said, "I have to tell you that when you asked us to work together, I was against it. But when Chris and I started working together, I realized he had a perspective and several key insights that I was missing. With a little trial and error, we were able to get this done ahead of schedule. We've even begun to plan some ways we can work together on the next assignment."

Mark smiled as he thought about how Dominic would be proud of his efforts to pull his team together, just like the trapeze team.

A few days later, Mark was at his desk when his phone rang. It was Dan, chairman of his university alumni society. Although a member of the group for years, Mark had rarely participated in the meetings, attending only one or two a year and helping out with the annual fund-raising barbecue.

After his talk with Victor about purpose in each ring, however, Mark had determined that a purpose for his self ring was to have a positive influence on his community.

He began attending alumni society meetings regularly and took a leadership role in one of their community service projects. He loved the challenge of helping people understand the need to be active in making their communities a better place to live and work.

Mark and Dan talked and joked about current events during their phone conversation. Then Dan said, "You know, Mark, several of us have been talking, and we think you would be a great candidate for president of the organization next year."

Mark was humbled and had an urge to say yes, but then recalled what Victor said about there being no room for another act in the circus.

"Dan, I'm flattered, but I must turn you down," he said. "I have too many things going on right now, and I would not be as focused on the position as I would need to be if I was elected.

"Lisa is just getting established in a new job, Jackie is starting school, and I've had a recent change here at work.

"I'll tell you what," he continued, "put me down as a candidate for the following year, and I'll plan ahead to fit it into my lineup."

"Lineup?" Dan asked.

Mark took a few moments to explain the concept of the three rings.

"So you see, Dan, I would really like to add serving as president as an act in one of my rings, but it's too big of a project to go into my lineup right now."

Although disappointed, Dan assured Mark he would keep him in mind for the following year. Mark hung up the phone and smiled because he had taken an important step toward keeping his circus lineup in order.

A Participant from the Audience

As Mark turned off his office lights and headed toward the stairs (no more elevator rides for him if it was four floors or less), he felt a sense of relief.

With his latest project complete and successfully implemented, he could take a much-needed break. The long weekend would be spent with Lisa and Jackie at a house in the mountains.

"No phones. No deadlines. My focus will definitely be on just two of my rings for the next few days," he thought.

Before reaching the stairway, he saw a light on in Greg's office. Greg was a manager in another department. Knowing that Greg was deep in the throes of a difficult project, he stopped by to lighten the moment with a little clown act.

Greg tried to laugh as Mark delivered his best joke, but stress prevented him from fully enjoying the moment.

"I just can't get my staff to commit more energy to the project," Greg explained. "I know they are overworked, but so am I. What is it they don't get?"

"Have you asked them?" Mark asked.

"Just come out and say, 'What can I do to help you commit?'" Greg retorted.

"Maybe not so forward," Mark replied, "but you have the right idea."

Mark sat down and pulled a piece of paper marked "professional ring" out of his briefcase. On it was drawn a large ring with the name of each member of Mark's department listed inside.

Mark talked with Greg about how he had worked individually with each member of his staff to better meet their needs at a time when he had placed tremendous demands on their time and energy.

For example, he allowed Ben to come into work an hour late so he could help his wife with their new baby. For Susan, who worked in the background, he had written "weekly praise" as a reminder to give positive feedback on her value to the project.

"What's this list under the word 'department' all about?" Greg asked.

"Those are things I did to take care of the team. One weekend, I invited all of the team members and their families to come to my house for dinner. Nothing elaborate, just a chance to get together, laugh, and relax. I even printed signs that read NO WORK DISCUSSIONS ALLOWED HERE to remind them why we were together.

"Another time, I rented a few lanes at the local bowling alley. We took a long lunch and enjoyed relieving our stress by pretending the bowling pins were frustrations."

"These are great ideas, Mark. You're a genius!" Greg replied.

"No, I was a general manager," Mark replied, recalling having met April during his visit to the circus a few months earlier.

"A what?" Greg asked, puzzled.

"Oh, nothing," Mark said.

Intermission

While at lunch one day in a local restaurant, Mark heard someone say, "So, Mark, still trying your juggling elephants routine?" The voice was unmistakable. A few tables over was Victor.

"My goodness," Mark said. "I saw the signs for the circus and thought of you and Dominic. But don't tell me you're spending your break here again this year. Really, Victor, you need to work on your self ring," Mark joked.

Victor laughed and said, "No, this is the year when my circus tours in this part of the country. So tell me, Mark, how is *your* circus?"

Intermission
is an essential
part of creating
a better circus
performance.

"Very good," Mark replied. "My team and I are more productive at work, and I haven't had a staff member leave in a year. I've lost seventeen pounds and even ran in a 5k for the first time in years. My relationship with Jackie has improved, too."

Victor noticed a touch of caution in Mark's voice.

"Wait a minute. Something is not quite right here," Victor said. "You have all these things going well. You should be on top of the world. What's wrong?"

"Well, to put it in circus terms," Mark confessed, "I feel like the audience is clapping, but I'm not getting any standing ovations. My life is good, but I just know it could be better."

Victor asked, "When was your last intermission?"

"Intermission?" Mark repeated.

"When was the last time you took some time off from your everyday acts?" Victor explained.

"I don't know," Mark replied. "I typically just keep choosing the most important ring to perform in, choose the right act, and get to work. Isn't that what you and Dominic taught me?"

"Yes," Victor replied, "but there's more to the circus than the acts in the lineup. **Intermission is an essential part of creating a better circus performance.**"

"Have you ever thought about why there is an intermission at the circus?" Victor asked.

What have you
done to improve
your performance
in one or more
of your rings?

"I would imagine it's to give the performers a break," replied Mark.

"That's partially correct," Victor said. "Why would an intermission benefit the audience as well?"

"Peanuts and hot dogs!" Mark replied with a laugh.

"Cute answer, Mark," said Victor. "But think about it. Intermission is a time for the audience to mentally relax, physically stretch, and be better prepared for the second half, whether it's a circus performance or a theater performance."

Victor continued. "One other point that may be helpful: Who have you invited to be in your audience lately?"

"OK, I have no clue where you are going with this one," Mark said.

Victor replied, "What I mean is, **What have you done to improve your performance in one or more of your rings?** Do you remember my reason for being at the circus last year?"

"I'm not sure I know what you mean," Mark said.

"I was on break when I met you at the circus, but Dominic had asked me to be there," Victor explained. "He wanted me to evaluate his performance and offer feedback."

"But Dominic is such an accomplished ringmaster," Mark said. "Why is feedback important to him?"

Your circus is
only as good
as your next
performance.

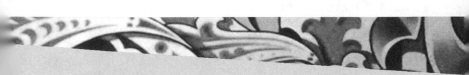

"One of Dominic's favorite sayings is, **'Your circus is only as good as your next performance.'** Dominic takes pride in knowing that last night's performance was good, but he wants to make sure that each time he serves as ringmaster, his performance is better than the last. He even asks for feedback from the audience."

"Would all this have anything to do with the people I saw talking with Dominic that day I stopped by the arena?" Mark asked.

"Yes," Victor said. "Those people had been in the audience during the week. They were asked to complete a survey on how the circus was doing as a total unit. Not just the acts, but the concessions, availability of information—anything that affected their experience at the circus."

"Such firsthand information gives us a good idea of our strengths and what we need to focus on improving for our next show or next year," Victor explained. "It all goes back to fulfilling our purpose."

"That seems like an enormous amount of work. Couldn't you just use your own personal evaluations to improve?" Mark asked.

"That's always a good place to start, but sometimes we are too close to really be objective," Victor replied, adding, "We need outside viewpoints from people who will give us honest feedback and even offer solutions, if possible."

"Has Dominic ever visited *your* circus?" Mark asked.

"Sure," Victor said. "Each time, he evaluated something different—the pace of the circus or how the performers interacted with the audience, for example."

"Do you ever have other people watch your circus?" Mark asked.

"Sure," Victor replied, "but not always as formally as in my evaluations from Dominic.

"For example, if I'm struggling with how to best describe an act, I talk with individuals who can help me craft the most effective wording.

"Last year, I attended a conference to learn how to more effectively handle change in my life," Victor recalled. "I picked up several powerful strategies that I still use today. And speaking of time," Victor said, "I hate to cut this short, but tonight is my first performance in your city. I would hate for the local papers to report, 'Acts are great, but ringmaster needs work.' "

"It was good to see you again, Victor," Mark said.

"Same here," Victor replied. "May all . . ."

Mark stopped him abruptly, "I know . . . May all your days be circus days!"

Victor laughed and said, "I think you would make a great ringmaster."

"I *am* a great ringmaster," Mark replied, "the ringmaster of my own circus."

Victor smiled in approval.

Change in the Program

As he finished his lunch, Mark reflected on Victor's words. He pondered the idea of an intermission and knew it would be helpful. He had been so busy concentrating on working *in* his life that he had not taken a step back to really look at how he could better work *on* his life.

Inviting people to help improve an area of his life was as exciting as it was scary. It reminded him of his high school coach, who always said, "You can never improve your game unless you play someone better than you."

Mark thought about a conversation he had with a close friend right after Jackie's birth. He and Lisa had always admired her and her husband's relationship with their children.

While he had not found every idea to be helpful, her insight on parenting techniques had helped him develop a better relationship with Jackie.

"I guess I'll have to find some other ringmasters to watch my circus," he thought. He finished his lunch and returned to work.

He thought about ways to gather feedback from his audience. His department had both internal and external customers. Mark scheduled the act of "focus on customer feedback" in his lineup. He would bring this up in his next department meeting and give the responsibility to someone on his team. He remembered Victor's words about not putting all the pressure on himself and delegating to get better results. "Delegate or die," he thought to himself.

Mark kept thinking about the idea of an intermission. "A time when I'm not actively working with my everyday acts. A time to reflect and renew." The idea was tempting, and the opportunity for such an event came sooner than he expected.

Mark had a regional managers meeting coming up in a few weeks on a Monday and Tuesday at a terrific coastal resort, and Lisa and Jackie already had plans to visit Lisa's mom the weekend prior to the meeting. Mark decided to make plans to drive to the resort on Friday evening and give himself an intermission.

After checking in and having dinner, he took a leisurely jog along the beach. At first, his thoughts turned to work and other things going on in his life, but he quickly reminded himself that the purpose of an intermission was to rest and renew his mental and physical energy.

Mark started focusing on the sound of the waves breaking on the shoreline and the feel of the night air. Doing so relieved much of the tension and anxiety he had been experiencing. He jogged a while longer before retiring to his room.

Mark awoke the next morning a little later than usual; the extra hour of sleep was just what he needed. He got dressed, grabbed his fishing gear from the car, and walked to the pier.

The morning sun was hanging over the horizon, and the weather was absolutely perfect. He couldn't remember when he had felt such a sense of renewed energy. The seagulls screeching, the scent of salt air, and the gentle breeze were refreshing. While fishing on the pier, he had no time constraints, no ringing phones, and no deadlines.

When he packed up his fishing gear a few hours later, Mark realized that thoughts about the acts in the three rings of his life were returning.

The intermission, however, had sharpened his focus and renewed his energy, so he welcomed the opportunity to fully engage in thinking about them.

Mark began his Sunday morning by reading the newspaper and enjoying a hot breakfast. After visiting a local church for worship, he took a walk along the beach.

Walking back to his room, Mark thought, "I believe I am ready to take my circus to the next level."

He took out his planning sheets from the past several months and started by simply reviewing the acts that had taken place. Reflecting on them made him smile.

"I have been so busy completing these acts that I haven't taken the time to step into the audience and appreciate the performance," he thought.

Mark turned his attention to the future, starting with his self ring because it was the one he most often neglected.

Reviewing his purpose for that ring, Mark listed some acts he would like to see over the next six to twelve months. He also considered which acts, if any, needed to be removed from his lineup, remembering that he could not do everything.

Before leaving his self ring, he began lining up the acts and briefly outlining ways to make each one successful. He completed the same process for his relationship ring.

His feeling of clarity about what he wanted to accomplish was energizing and he was excited about getting started on those acts. Once he'd finished his planning with the other two rings, Mark could focus more clearly on his professional ring.

He listed the acts that needed to be performed, then placed them in the lineup. Up next was the director's meeting.

He took extra time on this act, focusing on how he could acquire the skills to more efficiently accomplish the department's goals while engaging the strengths of each department member.

He finished planning, thinking to himself, "If I can make these acts successful in my circus, my boss and I will both be giving it a standing ovation."

The Monday meeting started in the usual way. A light breakfast on the patio was a great opportunity to catch up with other managers.

As much as Mark was ready to focus his energy on the primary agenda of the meeting, he knew that this was a time for him to be in his relationship ring as much as it was for him to be in his professional ring.

He focused on getting to know the new managers and renewing relationships with the others.

It wasn't long after the meeting started that the positive effects of Mark's intermission began to reveal itself. While some managers wanted to use the time to gripe about past failures, a refreshed Mark was offering objective insights about both the successes and shortcomings of his department.

In their afternoon brainstorming session, Mark outlined the two key strategies that he believed would help the company to be more successful next year, and then asked for feedback.

While some seemed skeptical, everyone was pleasantly surprised when Mark was able to show how the strategies could be integrated into the company's three-year plan by combining his initial ideas with feedback from the group.

As the meeting ended, a senior vice president shook Mark's hand and said, "Mark, you and I have been coming to these meetings for years. Normally, you show up, make your report, and that's about it.

"Today you were different," he continued. "At any point in the meeting, I could see you were fully engaged in what was being discussed.

"You gave us two really good Ideas for the company and led the discussion on how to improve and implement them. My only question is, 'What changed?'"

"Well, let's just say I've spent some time getting my act together," Mark replied, thinking about the value of an intermission.

"Whatever you're doing," he said with a smile, "keep it up. We need more leaders like you in our organization."

"There's one standing ovation already," Mark thought as he headed for his car.

A New Level of Performance

Returning home, Mark put one of his ideas into action immediately. The very next day at work, he stopped by to see George, the most successful manager in the company. After exchanging some pleasantries, he got down to business.

"George, I know you are busy, but I could really use your help. I have always been impressed with your ability to align the skills of your team to constantly changing assignments and priorities.

"My next project is going to be a nightmare," Mark explained. "I was wondering if you could give me some strategies on how you would approach it."

George seemed flattered.

"Mark, I would be glad to show you what I know, if you really think it would be helpful," he said.

Mark thanked him for his willingness to help and set up a time to take George to lunch.

During his intermission, Mark had also reflected on the need to begin working on an advanced degree if he wanted to move up in the company. He contacted three friends who had taken a similar career path and asked each of them about their experience and what they would change if they had the chance to do it all over again. The information he gained prevented Mark from making the costly mistake of choosing the wrong degree program or graduate school.

One personal issue that weighed on his mind during intermission was a recent conversation he had with his wife, Lisa. They had discussed the possibility of having a second child. Mark and Lisa both wanted more children, but with their rings already full, they just didn't know how they would manage the huge change.

To get some help in this ring, Mark and Lisa talked with dual-career friends who had more than one child. They asked questions such as "How do you deal with the extra responsibility?" and "How do you find time for each other and the children, while still being able to focus on your jobs?"

Again, their insight was invaluable. Mark and Lisa also took advantage of the opportunity to participate in a retreat to help strengthen their marriage.

Mark took a more proactive approach to his own needs. He started getting regular physical checkups and, for a brief time, even secured the services of a personal trainer. He scheduled time for fishing, hiking, and several rounds of golf with friends.

One day while looking for something in his desk drawer, Mark came across the program from the circus he and Jackie had attended almost three years earlier. He smiled as he recalled that first meeting with Victor.

I was just too busy trying to juggle elephants, he thought. Mark vowed never again to forget that he was the ringmaster of his own circus and to get the most important things done.

After
the Story

The Grand Finale

As Mark stepped off the stairs, he wondered if Jackie had finished reading the story. More important, he wondered if she had gotten anything out of it.

"She probably already called Lisa and told her I have a secret fantasy of joining the circus," he thought.

Opening the door to his office, Mark saw Jackie busily writing.

"Still think I'm crazy?" he asked.

"If you are, then put me in the same category," she answered, holding up a sheet of paper.

Mark sat down next to Jackie and looked at the paper. It was strangely familiar.

"What are you doing?" he asked.

"Working on my lineup," Jackie answered.

"Dad, you know how independent I can be.

"I have always tried to deal with my problems on my own and take pride in being able to work things out.

"When I walked into your office earlier today, I really needed help. The last place I expected to find it was in a recollection of your experience with a circus performance.

"Dad, your story is fantastic. I can really relate to many of the things you talk about. It is the greatest gift you could give me right now."

"How so?" Mark replied.

"The first idea that really hit home was how the ringmaster has the greatest influence on the success of the circus.

"I had been looking at my situation and feeling like a victim, helpless to change," Jackie recounted. "That part made me realize that for things to improve, I have to take control rather than let my circumstances control me. Markets will change and my boss will always expect more of me. What I have to do is use those circumstances as a stepping stone for my actions, not a stumbling block.

"I now see that it's impossible to get everything done. So, as I plan the rest of my week in the office, I'm focusing more on what acts *should* be in the ring and how to make them successful. One thing I want to make happen soon is an intermission for the staff."

"Good idea," Mark said.

"It would be so helpful for my team right now," Jackie replied. "We have been so drained lately because of our workload. If we had a few hours together to do something other than focus on our next deadline, it would energize us to be more engaged when we return to work."

"I also feel like we could really benefit from changing how we gather feedback from our customers to more accurately determine how we are doing and how we can improve. This will help us better determine our priorities and should reduce some of the stress related to work overload."

"I hope you don't mind, Dad," Jackie said, "but I would like to take your story and make copies of it. There are people at work who could use it right now."

"I'm flattered," Mark responded.

Jackie continued. "One person who will definitely get a copy is Blake. He works so hard, but sometimes on the wrong things. By the end of the day, he's frustrated. I think he will really connect with the part of the story about acts serving a purpose and focusing on the right things."

Jackie laughed and added, "I can see him now, looking at his to-do list, marking things off, saying, 'This act does not belong in my circus.'

"Another person I might give the story to is Wendy, our vice president of marketing. She has such a passion to see her department succeed. However, her last few productions have not gone very well. The part in the story about the need for acts to begin and end at different times should help her see the need to manage her projects and resources more effectively."

"And the third copy?" Mark asked.

"That's for the next person I meet who is trying to juggle elephants," she answered. "It's so easy to let yourself get overwhelmed trying to get everything done and meet all the expectations you create for yourself… and that others put on you.

"Pretty soon, you either feel like some part of your life is going to crash down like an elephant you actually threw into the air, or you see your situation as impossible.

"The story is a simple and fun way to recognize current challenges and discover practical tools to accomplish what is really important, both at work and in your personal life. At the same time, the concepts deliver a deeper message that is so urgently needed in a world of endless opportunities and distractions."

Jackie stood up and hugged her dad.

"Speaking of getting things done, I need to start heading home," she said. "I have a feeling, though, that there will be many more circus discussions over the next few months. Thanks for taking me to the circus . . . again," she said, gesturing with the story in her hand.

"My pleasure," Mark said. "The circus will be back in the spring. Why don't we plan on going again, just you and me. That should really bring the concepts to life. I'll even buy the peanuts."

"You've got a deal," Jackie replied, laughing. "Until then, I'll just let your story be my food for thought as I get my acts together."

With another quick hug, Jackie left her dad's office and headed home.

Let the Performance Begin!

Now It's Time to
Get Your Act Together!

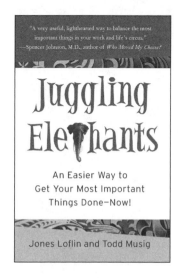

To learn more about products
and services for individuals and
organizations based on
Juggling Elephants,
visit:
www.jugglingelephants.com
or call:
1-800-853-4676

You can also get information about discounted bulk sales at
www.jugglingelephants.com.

Penguin's Business-to-Business Advantage program allows your
local bookstore to offer special discounted pricing on this title for
bulk sales. Your business, school, non-profit, or church can receive
special discounted pricing, great service, direct shipping, and more.
Call your local bookstore and say you'd like to use Penguin's B2B
program to buy copies of this book for giveaway or training.

_____ *Juggling Elephants* 978-1-591-84171-5 $19.95 ($25.00 CAN)

the life all around me
by Ellen Foster

Kaye Gibbons

✦ ✦ ✦

the life all around me
by Ellen Foster

HARCOURT, INC.

Orlando   Austin   New York   San Diego   Toronto   London

www.HarcourtBooks.com

Library of Congress Cataloging-in-Publication Data
Gibbons, Kaye, 1960–
The life all around me by Ellen Foster/Kaye Gibbons.—1st ed.
p.   cm.
1. Teenage girls—Fiction.   2. Foster home care—Fiction.
3. Poetry—Authorship—Fiction.   4. North Carolina—Fiction.
I. Title.
PS3557.I13917L54 2006
813'.54—dc22   2005014552
ISBN-13: 978-0151-01204-6   ISBN-10: 0-15-101204-0

Text set in Fournier MT
Designed by Cathy Riggs

Printed in the United States of America

First edition
A C E G I K J H F D B

For Barbara Sue Atkins Allen Batts
The town lady with all the names,
Who prefers life and fabric textured.
And
For my daughters, Mary, Leslie, and Louise,
Why and how I do this.
And with all thanks to Connie May Fowler,
Who led me to Joy Harris,
Who led me to Ann Patty,
Who led to this, this next one, the one after that . . .

President Derek C. Bok   September 20, 1974
Harvard University
Cambridge, Massachusetts

Dear President Bok,

My name is Ellen Foster. I hope this finds you happy, in good health, and thriving in picturesque New England. It is not quite as scenic here in my part of North Carolina, also known as Variety Vacationland, but this is because I live in the flat, blank section between the Atlantic Ocean and the Great Smokey Mountains, which team up to account for the Variety.

One of my mottoes is that nothing you think, feel, or do should be watered down, so when I decided to try out for college, Harvard sounded like the only place to be. The main reason I'm returning my information to you instead of the correct office is because there happen to be some things off the average about me and I needed to make sure you know they're reality. Wanting to start Harvard at only fifteen could seem like a tale, for example, but it's true and I believe it makes sound sense because of all the surplus living that was jammed into the years.

My childhood was the kind that saturates you with quick ambition to think through and begin the next episode of your life, although I've been trying to seize each day and appreciate it more as is. A compare and contrast would be trying to break the trend of picking through oranges and handling them until you believe you've finally come across the perfect example to taste. Those years also made me into an individual who wouldn't be disdone by the large experience of leaving my road to go learn amid ten thousand or so older strangers, not to say anything is currently the matter. Everything has definitely been on the up in up, but even if I was trying to escape pressing hardship at home or a checkered reputation at school, I wouldn't select Harvard to go on the lam.

A person who graduated from there was supposed to grade how close I come to being Harvard material, and I need to let you know I went to town to meet the man we

have, but when I got to his nursing home I found him un-
aware. He'd had another stroke the day before and is now
locked in a state of deep coma, but if another one crops
up before the deadline, I'll get them to create an opinion
and send it to you immediately. The bookmobile librarian
who told me about the man is keeping her eyes peeled, but
for now, I'd appreciate it if you could please allow this letter to count toward the missing point of view.

If the man had been able to ask why I felt motivated
toward Harvard, I would've said I want to be exposed to
harder teachers who have strict yet interesting requirements and a student body that thrives on curiosity. It'd be
fascinating to be in a lunchroom with people sharing information about simple miracles, such as the smallpox
and hookworm vaccinations, or having someone speak
up and tell about a family vacation to Crete. In fact, my
goal is to study both English and medicine and then enter
the field of epidemic disease research. I see myself going
into the wilds of places like Bali or Tahiti to research folk
customs of medical cures and deliver vaccines as well as
lessons on both nutrition and poetry.

To reach this ideal, what I believe I need to do now
is go ahead and enter a future where people share a love
of living more in the mind and see a value in studying

things that never sound required for survival on the surface, such as how Socrates talked with his philosophical pupils. I can only imagine the daily awe of learning while surrounded by marble columns featuring the sayings of Aristotle, Homer and others, New England fall foliage, and perhaps some flying buttresses. It sounds urgent, but it's only because the best time to leave is almost here. The present situation is I'm at the threshold of completing nine years at my rural school and crossing the real and symbolic road to enter the high school. I could easily turn toward town and the train station instead, where the map says the train lets out a very walkable sliver of distance from Harvard, unless a night arrival or books I may need to bring in the baggage make it wiser to flag a taxi for the campus dormitory or female rooming house, depending on what each would be asking.

Going on to the brief narration of my background section, I need to let you know not to read mine and think this girl's trying to create a mood of shock and sympathy to gain a free ride or discount. The summary is that my mother became too sad and died when I was nine, and ordinary life got and stayed unusual for the two years it took to track down the steady foster situation I still enjoy here. Things in between include moving out of the house due to my father's problems and then his death due to a sudden head vein explosion the next year, living with an aunt who didn't have raising another girl in mind, living with my art teacher and then getting moved out of there because of judicial branch confusion, getting assigned to live with my grandmother who soon sickened, lingered, and died, loving school as well as close friends throughout, reading like a fiend, having to move out of another house on Christmas and walking up the road to the house of girls run by a foster lady, thus my name Ellen Foster.

If I had the job of selecting a well-rounded group of individuals to come to my college, I would worry about an underage orphan with a list of obstacles showing up and being a misfit, but I want to emphasize that I get along well both at school and at home. My foster mother is not pleased with my educational outlook and has tried to correct it on this end, but the private school here is the Academy of the New Dawn Apocalypse, and the school board said forced busing was enough upheaval so they cannot allow students to bend the rules to skip grades or change schools, unless a person needs Braille material or rails. When I asked her about Harvard, she said she'd seen college careers pan out for several piano and mathematical prodigies on public television, so nothing would be lost by me giving it a try with only offering more general skills of the mind. I realize that it could not be more expensive, which is why I need to emphasize that I know how to work and don't at all mind it.

On a typical morning at Harvard, for example, I could put in a few hours at the cafeteria, working the breakfast tray line, or at the gym, handing out baskets, although I have more experience in the library. I've been trained in all areas from ordering from the state depository to changing bulletin boards and worked in there alone for the three months of the librarian's knee surgery and malpractice case, and as she is now wheelchair bound and so much of a library involves reaching, I catch her up on a range of her daily duties. If you do not have the Dewey decimal system, I'd quickly adapt to your procedure. There's also the school store and canteen, and I've worked in the concession stand at high school sports games and during a series of wrestling extravaganzas in town and Billy Graham crusade shows.

Besides the current weekend jobs in home and church cleaning and magazine sales, I collect and write the school news, which runs each Saturday. It pays next to nothing, although everybody says the savings I can put toward Harvard from the cleaning, the food service, and magazines would pay for an ordinary education, if that's what I was after. I enclosed a copy of my column, Ellen's Tellin, to check on the possibility of getting on at the paper up there. One last idea is although I understand Harvard doesn't have a special education section, I wanted to let you know that I could substitute teach in the neighborhood for all types of unruly people based on my experience monitoring special students during their teacher's rest period.

Overall, it wouldn't be a problem for me to put in forty hours per week and also maintain top grades and participate in some extracurricular activities, such as intellectual clubs, debating leagues, and public speaking. I've been able to compete in speaking and would like to continue. Enclosed is the essay from the 1974 Woodmen of the World Youth Public Speaking contest which won in my state and then in Washington DC, entitled, Franklin Delano Roosevelt: King Arthur or Robin Hood? There was so much to send, I decided not to send the other one that won with the medical auxiliary entitled, Marie Curie: Madam and Mother, but I went ahead and enclosed The Cell Wall and the Surface of Hemingway's Stories: A Compare and Contrast, which won a scholarship to the humanities program Johns Hopkins in Baltimore puts on this October.

In closing, I hope everything helps show that I wouldn't be a fade-out or a person who turns to drink or dope when things become tough. I believe that anything is possible if you have the combination of love for what you're doing and the will to sit down and not get up until it's done. I realize the amount of work ahead and the costs, and even though the only scholarship plan I know about at this time is the one sponsored by the United Negro College Fund, which I am not eligible for with just the problem of being this young, I do have a mind, which we all agree is a terrible thing to waste.

Your friend,
Ellen Foster

One

ANYONE CONSIDERING MAKING AN UNDERAGE change in life, such as who you're going to live with, should know there's no way to avoid the government getting in on the decision, so try to be kind to the lady they'll send with a stack of tests and try to stay calm and do your best on them. I moved in here three years ago on Christmas Day of 1971, knowing as I knocked on the door that I was choosing this particular replacement for life with my mother because the foster mother, Laura, had the kind of home you'd be out of your mind not to settle into for good.

Kaye Gibbons

My family was either dead or crazy, so there wasn't
the fall-back of concerned loved ones. In fact, my
mother's sister, Nadine, who looks sane in public, had
created a no-room-at-the-inn situation during her and
her daughter Dora's festivities that caused me to strike
out walking for Laura's house.

The next summer Laura notified the government that
all was well and they could go ahead and draw up her
parental rights paperwork. Lo and behold a letter arrived
to say Social Service was fine with our arrangement as
long as I could pass the mental stability tests meant to
prove whether I was too much of a damaged goods personality to live with a nice individual permanently or if I
needed to be demoted into a more routine nightmare orphan home.

When Laura noticed me at the kitchen table with the
letter and a resuscitated nail-biting habit, she said, You
can't prepare for tests like these, Ellen, and when I called
to say it's been nothing but a joy having you here, and I
think I'd know by now if I needed to be sleeping with my
eyes open because you were across the hall plotting wak-
ing nightmares, the woman said the tests were manda-
tory but they're a formality. There's nothing to worry

10

about unless you chew your fingers so far down you can't write the answers.

She took me in for the tests the following Saturday morning, and just as I made the last multiple choice decision on whether I'd rather watch television or play baseball the lady told Laura and me to pardon the surprise but I needed to be shut up alone for another two hours with a kind of raw intelligence test they tacked on to the mental health portion. I said it was fine, just let me go to the bathroom and sharpen my pencil, not mentioning my suspicion that this was a fresh trick.

Laura took a breath and quietly blew her words out toward the lady, telling her in a way that could sound rude if you don't imagine it correctly, Well, she's here. She's willing and more than capable. I know the government's always created a certain amount of make-work, but it's worrisome for you to double tests that don't matter.

The lady said every time the court decided a child's life, the individual had to be run through particular tests before they could more or less turn you out into a new future. Pardon her again for not telling us about yet another final detail sooner, but a letter would be coming with instructions on when and where to take me for a thorough physical, courtesy of the government, down to the eyes, ears, and teeth.

She was smiling, hopeful we'd appreciate a free medical visit, but Laura blew gently again, saying, I'll take care of it. We have a family doctor. Shouldn't my fitness as a parent be a concern?

Laura wasn't being conceited, only picturing us in a line of teenage mothers with babies on their hips sucking root beer out of blue plastic milk bottles. Sorry to say it but I filled out that scene in the bathroom. When I got back and saw Laura running my pencils through a motorized sharpener, her tight method of movement and the way she dashed back her hair made her favor Ava Gardner, definite-edged in the midst of murky people, like in The Night of the Iguana when she's managing the old maid and the traveling women. The lady was fixated on Laura. She hadn't answered Laura yet, but she finally said, You can take her to the Mayo Clinic if you want to, and we know you're more than fit to take permanent custody of Ellen. How many pencils does she need?

More than she was led to believe, Laura told her, but since this is the last time, I'll let it be, and hope she'll be ready when I come for her. You know, it's Saturday.

She didn't say she was aggravated that the second test made us miss Willy Wonka and interrupted her plan to help catch me up on ordinary events by taking me to one childhood-type movie a month. She was aware of how when I was little, we stayed inside the house. The thought of heading out to the matinee movies or the family drive-in theater never arose due to different extremes. Now it was another thing available just to get up and go do. After American Bandstand, after the other two foster girls and I ate some sandwiches off the fold-out tables, we'd make the first afternoon showing and then walk around downtown, eating hot dogs and window shopping.

After the tests, Laura let me in the car, not all there, mumbling to me, And I'm even sorrier the downtown theater's switching over from Willy Wonka to Art Garfunkel, of all people, in something you can't see and I don't want to. We need another theater. Who here would buy a ticket to watch Art Garfunkel with his clothes off?

I said, It's okay about missing the movie. They'll probably bring it back on the summer daytime schedule next year.

But you'll be too old for it then, she said. I'm aware you already are, but I thought it was important. How do you think you did on the tests?

I told her fine but draining, so I probably would've passed out in the theater. She said, Well, it's worked out for the best I suppose. We've got ten miles of straight road home if you want to rest your head in my lap.

I was sore from tensing in a hard chair for so long and didn't feel like touching right then, but I didn't want her to take it as I was upset about the movie and do the kind of out of her way thing she was prone to do and suggest we follow it to the next town. I was also guilty from being relieved I didn't have to sit through Willy Wonka and come out jangled up after two hours of watching overly eager singers and have to fix my face to say I'd just had a red-letter time of my life. Sweaty and sticky candy factory children hopping and singing around the chocolate vats, like they just happen to be living out the words to the songs, could irk you. I get more of a bang out of stories of realism that take place in the house or in the city, nothing on the open range, no forest or jungle except for Heart of Darkness, and except for Moby Dick, no man versus nature.

I was glad to feel her fingers on my hair though when I remembered the dark undersoul Willy Wonka had in the book and wondered if they'd allowed enough of him in the movie that you'd come out nervous about opening candy bars. People my age are old enough to know better, but I know some on my road, including myself, who're jubus about unwrapping a new cake of soap because of the nightmare possibility of seeing an innocent, trapped face staring up at you, permanently pressed there after a bad snatched hostage ordeal at Old Soap Molly's house. If you've lived a certain way and already have a lasting set of damages, you avoid what frightening fantasies you can.

It was only ten miles, but the weight of Laura's hand on my head and the tires underneath us knocked me out. I went straight to bed and just as I fell away, I was jerked back by the idea that the government was an expert at making you wait. I was facing another span of time I'd had to get to the other side of, not live wholly inside. After a month had passed, Laura called the Social Service lady, who said she couldn't help the backup, but remember the tests were only formalities. I wanted to shout and ask her if she'd ever needed permission to call her home a home or been jolted out of ease she'd trusted would come because the world couldn't possibly keep turning the wrong way. I pictured her arriving on the scene when I was too far past my ability to endure it and wreck what there was left of the life I'd reduced to reading with bleeding eyes and crawling to the supper table and crying on a pallet in the Easy Reader section of the library at school.

Laura would lean against the refrigerator, on the phone with my friends' mothers telling different versions of how tragic it was to watch me wait and what lengths she was tempted to go to if she didn't need to set a patient and legal example for me and the two other girls living with us, who started behaving like I was on their nerves for more than being odd now. Although Laura was evenhanded, they saw favoritism everywhere. There was nothing I could do except stay off to myself and do only the most basic portions of living the grouped-together life while they slid farther and farther downhill from the high state of niceness they seemed to enjoy when I'd moved in.

Laura explained that it was part of my nature to work off steam doing things like chattering about the tests and cleaning what wasn't dirty, and they needed to respect what the basic notion of being tested meant to me. She told them, We all have a way we'd prefer people to see us, and Ellen's very conscious of her abilities and nervous about a judgment made about them the same way I'd be uncomfortable if somebody suddenly decided to measure my ability to run a house, the same way you'd be if you had to jump through hoops before your families, well, something large like that, could, well, be sorted out. Laura left the room quickly, with everybody understanding the three of them weren't close enough for her to open up the can of worms on the wicked predicaments they'd been in. She tended to them well and hoped it helped, knowing she couldn't mention their histories and fates without one of them defending the kind of person and behavior that deserved nothing. They stayed shut up together, blowing and sullen. I overheard them wondering if I'd have to leave if I failed, saying compared and contrasted to them I had it made with a dead family and an unknown future. Their mood improved when it dawned on one that at least they'd have the freedom to roam once they were out from under Laura's roof. You'd think they would've sympathized with my fears of getting dragged off to some gnashing-teeth type of place and suffering to sleep on a spotted mattress, hunched over, holding my tennis shoes and clean socks with the blue dingleballs from getting robbed off my feet by some bloodthirsty orphans.

Finally, the lady got here and got to the point pretty immediately, saying that figuring out what to do about me had taken more time than she'd expected because they'd graded the tests twice and then had to consider more complicated plans after my IQ popped up in the range where people are prone to losing their ration and nursing along gibberish plots to overthrow the government. Then she wanted to stress that my destiny could also simply be nonproductive.

Laura said, Okay then, we need to put this news, such as it is, toward making the rest of her life better than it's been. It sounds simple, but it isn't. You know what I mean? But this has to mean she can stay. Am I right?

Yes, the lady said, and what Ellen needs to realize her full potential involves nothing you can't handle, although I've had some troubling doubts about her school. The prisons are filled with people who dipped and dipped and then dallied out of boredom, so if she's dissatisfied with a particular class or drifting, she can study that subject independently in the library, one or two or all of them, whatever works best.

It was only Mrs. Delacroix in the library, and even though she'd gladly give you her all, that didn't come out to too much. She'd run the lunchroom until she suffered mistakes during a leg vein operation, so now she was bound to a wheelchair and waiting for a lawyer to make her doctor pay for destroying her ambulation. She had a different way of speaking she chalked up to Louisiana, and although I loved listening to her, you don't want somebody stewing their language around taking a stab at training you for college. I explained some concerns, such as the only book Mrs. Delacroix had read was The Power of Positive Thinking, and me being left to wander around unorganized in so much information and asked whether help was coming from anywhere else. The lady described more about the lesson plans for self-guided people in my category and said she'd explained all this to the principal. There'd also be bottomless advice available from the college education teachers who'd drawn up the guidelines.

Fighting not to see myself reclused in with Mrs. Delacroix, changing her leaking vein bandages and accumulating nervous isolation tics, I told her I got along with people very well and had been going around with the same group from my road since we started to school. I wasn't the kind who slopes around and eats lunch alone. You wouldn't see me, I told her, and say I look lonesome.

She swore this wouldn't cut me off from civilization, and I'd be able to do as much or as little as I wanted to do extracurricularly. Then looking at Laura, the lady said, Ellen's imagination's getting away with her, and that's part of what we've been mindful to keep satisfied.

Pardon me, Laura told her, but even if it was possible to keep someone with such a high curiosity entirely occupied, I don't think the goal of giving Ellen what she needs should be to keep her out of trouble, which she's shown no inclination to get into anyway.

She told Laura she agreed it was miraculous I'd stayed free of delinquencies, and then she handed me the stack of outline materials and the court papers which had been stamped to approve me permanently. Our first job is to see to the body and the mind, she said, and I think it's safe to say that between your new situation at school and this wonderful home, you should flourish, but I want to remind you that to whom much is given, much is expected.

I had to ask, Who expects it? How much is much?

Sighing so long and hard the wind almost knocked me down, she said, Ellen, you need to consider how fortunate you are. You need to thank your living God to be alive and well and blessed with the extraordinary good sense He gave you, and if you're ever called upon to endure again, I trust, after everything you've been through, you'll be the kind of young woman who will suffer gladly.

So, that was it, I told Laura. I never have to peel the back of my legs off government seating again.

To celebrate, she had an outsized, overly stuffed floral chair I'd tried out downtown delivered to the corner of my room, and for the next three years, if you were looking for me in the house, if I wasn't in the kitchen or Laura's room, I was in the Mamie Eisenhower chair, reading books from the library the handyman veteran installed in the living room after the college education office told Laura about ordering used books from the mail-order professor's catalog. There's a ladder leaned against the shelves, not on roller wheels on a gold bar, just the one the man left behind after Laura mistakenly paid him in full before he'd finished the final touches. We made it match by stripping off the paint drips and spills and staining it the New England home library deep tone of chocolate.

Two

THE SYSTEM WAS FINE FOR THE FIRST TWO YEARS. Then last year Holden Caulfield began eating worry into me about whether I wanted to go through with crossing the road to the regular rural high school, which would be for all intents and purposes my old school but with ashtrays outside the main hall. I knew I couldn't keep up with Holden and his crowd on matters such as clothing and leather luggage, but competing for grades didn't seem that difficult. I had the advantage of a history of working like a dog while they seemed to give themselves a great deal of time off for sports and touring dates around New York City.

I made sure to thank Laura for everything she'd done before I went into her bedroom one evening and sprung on her how I needed more. She had house and family magazines spread around, and when she shoved them over for me to sit down and tell her what I needed, I had to say that all I knew was I was feeling more and more squirmy about spending three years at a school with everybody whose ambitions were lowered down to just the rural style of life. Since the only choice of private education was the Apocalypse school, I didn't know what to do about this sensation that my future was being threatened into impossible.

She more than understood and said she'd call the Social Service lady the next morning, but for now, if I wanted a view into a world where too much of a good thing spelled more trouble than having nothing, I should crawl up with her and read an article on the swanky home life of Patty Hearst. You can't watch Citizen Kane accumulate his trove and not picture yourself ringing the doorbell at Xanadu and having him quiz you on your various interests and needs before he laughs heartily and says he's been waiting for someone like you and he'd be honored if you'd allow him to set you up in a fabulous dormer room and keep you in clothes his magazines advertise and then send you to college well-versed in conversation.

The government fell short of a situation Citizen Kane and the modern Hearst crowd could set you up in, but at least the lady came quickly this time. When Laura phoned her up, she'd alerted her to bring the next height of ideas, and so she splayed out what she'd investigated into across the kitchen table, pointing to brochures on different talent camps and weekend college seminars, lining out what they could cover on fees and transportation and what we had to pay, using the tone you associate with the man listing the prices of soybean and pork belly futures on the news. The figures could be shaking up Idaho, but not to hear him tell it. The difference was the lady was talking about sums that can alter your life, and I didn't know whether her mind had come unconnected from her mouth and words like, well over a thousand, meant nothing to her, or, if she looked around at our stuff and style and assumed we had that kind of money casually lying around in the black box with stars lacquered on to it, which actually did look perfect for holding strong-smelling stacks of new cash. Laura was also behaving like a pod person, taking in the news with no expression, nodding some, taking notes, I was scratching, chewing, sucking, blowing, sweating, and pulsing, barely able to sputter out, I had no idea I was turning out to be this expensive. Do they have some variety of greenbacks stamp deal or a coupon book like the chamber of commerce has for holiday hotels and rent-a-cars? I'm sorry, but something has told me these IQ camps ran more in the thirty, forty dollar range.

Why, the lady asked, would you think that?

I said, money and the mind usually seem to live so far apart, and I'm sorry, but you expect Harvard to be priced this high, but not weekends with the chess crowd. I really thought you'd go off on what this one brochure's making sound like a brain isolation retreat and rough it more on the cheap, but it quotes you between six and eight hundred dollars to sleep in the sand dunes and fight fleas and get up at the crack of dawn to operate on fish.

This one, Laura said, in Baltimore, this humanities program sounds custom-made for you. It's next October at Johns Hopkins.

A wave of sick faintness I hadn't felt in a while washed through me. I'd wanted to be through with the kind of hot, crackling black coming down over my eyes like a shade shot through with pierces of light. I needed to droop to the floor before another wave came down or to get to the bathroom somehow to press my face against the tile and wait for the acids to stop churning up and melting the tender tissues inside my throat. Laura reached for my hands. There was security in knowing she recognized a mood coming on and wouldn't allow me to pass out and die from a sharp blow to the head on the way down, but I didn't want her to comment on how cold and clammy I was and have Social Service panic over my well-being.

I clamped my hands between my knees and spoke quietly to keep my stomach less disturbed, only partway hearing myself over questions screaming inside me, asking if I was ever going to heal from the plague of frustrations. Other people don't have to chew up good time recovering nor see their hearts throbbing through their undershirts because the person who committed to caring for them promised to do what it takes to give them something they need.

Laura, I said, it's okay, and thank you, but a weekend in Baltimore runs about what I thought college costs. It's too much. Actually, it's way too much.

Laura said, Well, this is a new world I'm in now, but you seem to get what you pay for there, so don't worry.

When the lady said educational money was easily had from civic groups that doted on ambitious youth, another wave of the blues washed through me. I could see Laura sitting on the sofa, shivering with blankets around her shoulders while her bathwater's boiling in a pot she's had to hang by the fireplace, going without to repay the debt I'd caused by spending like the wind at a high-IQ camp. I said, Mam, I think those are all ideas, but it isn't like we're part of the have-nots, and when you get down to the reality of it, taking a train or a plane for a weekend at a famous college isn't the kind of thing I have any business doing.

Laura said, Ellen, didn't you see these brochures?

I said, I did, and everything looks interesting, but I'll be fine with the way things are at school. This other's too different, it's too all-out. It's for people who do things like spending a thousand dollars on clothes, but I appreciate the thought. If we found a pearl in some oysters or won the Kentucky Derby, then I'd be more able to do it.

The lady had been sopping her cookies in her coffee and eating them all over her lips to where you regretted offering them to her, but she'd been doing that a while. Then, after I was through talking, she stopped and dotted her mouth with a napkin saying, Well, this is certainly a changed you I'm hearing. Three years ago, the little girl I tried to talk to was so hostile and defensive she wouldn't have given me air in a jug.

Laura said, I don't think it's necessary to make it sound like she was ruthless back then, though if it seemed that way, you can bet it was the best she could do. I didn't get her here, the government certainly didn't. Her attitude is why we're sitting here now. You know I know from ruthless children, you've certainly sent more than my quota to me.

The lady put her saucer at the edge of the table and shoved her crumbs over into it, keeping her head down, so she wouldn't move on toward the subject Laura had just come very close to, of how I'd had to strong-arm the other two girls back into the foster care system when they finally caused more chaos than Laura and I could stand earlier in the year. She left without mentioning it, saying on the way out the door only to remember her old advice about much being expected from those who were given as much as I'd been blessed with. Although she worded it differently, she ended by saying she trusted that two people as clever as Laura and me could figure out how to get me off this road if we believed I was so

different I required special and high-tone surroundings
to fulfill my destiny in.

While I was putting the program brochures away in
the rolltop desk Laura kept household paperwork in, I
opened my savings passbook and told her what I had thus
far wouldn't cover cake decorating classes at the night
college over by the lumber mill. Then I closed the top
and lay on the sofa and gazed at cartoons, waiting for my
stomach to cool down. She pulled a blanket over my legs
and began going through the house and rambling for
things that needed to be washed or hit with the iron a second time. She finished sooner than usual, and there she
stood by my feet, screeching the ironing board open and
plugging in the iron and holding her hands around it
while it warmed, favoring Ava Gardner again when she's
holding on to the handlebar of the rolling cocktail-hour
cart and converting it into a steadying symbolic rock.

Laura always called for me to come spit on the iron
because she knew I liked hearing it sizzle, but when she
offered, my stomach didn't feel right enough to be up.
When I told her I needed to lie there and feel like dirt a
few more minutes, she said, I know you do.

I said, I don't want to be smart-mouthed, but you
know I didn't come here with a dowry. I brought one

hundred and sixty-six dollars in a paper sack, and that's earned about a dollar in interest since then. If I were you I'd be relieved if somebody said they were willing to stay home for free.

I believe you'll get a scholarship, she said, but if you didn't or if it isn't enough, we'll figure something out. Any number of things can be done, so at the very least, I want you to plan on going to this program.

I said, And when you fall into deep debt to pay for my college and I fall in front of a bus and can't work to repay you so you can repay the bank, ask me if I hadn't seen it coming every time the collector drove off with my father's late-payment merchandise. We have some interesting stories already going on here, and I don't see any plots that involve you living in more or less a drainage tube in Calcutta because of me. You know I have to go by the theme of working to get the money you need for something. It's a simple if-then, Laura. If you did that, you can do this. I don't see how it varies from you always getting up and doing the nastiest job of the day first.

Moving my legs aside to sit down, she said, Getting the best education possible isn't like bleaching grout. And listen when I tell you, a girl your age has no business thinking about death and taxes. Repaying me for this course or the others or college or anything, Ellen, shouldn't occur to you. I'd expect some gratitude, being human I suppose, but that's the extent of it, so if it doesn't concern me, there's no reason for it to grind you this way.

The only problem is you don't realize how dangerous it could be to take what you offer. They said I wasn't damaged, but this is damage, this is a mess I've brought to your house, only you don't consider it the selfish way I would if I were you. I can fix this. You'll stay glad I'm here, but not if I take what's yours. I know how to get what I need done. It's real and true and simpler like this.

She rubbed a circle on my leg and patted the place down before she hopped up and unplugged the iron. Looking at the television, she said, I didn't know they were running Dark Shadows again. I've seen you watch that, so just rest with it and I'll come iron later.

Laura asked for nothing but the honor of having a girl like me, to look after and hold her daily conversations and customs with. When I considered the harm I could do Laura, it was embarrassing, revolting, and much more horrible than the idea of her paying for my education. There was the force to feel the wind off of, the sting of a slap from a person too turned in on herself to rehearse how the wounds would feel and too familiar with them to stop and measure their speed and imagine the surprise someone like Laura must feel each time she closed herself in her room to adjust herself to it, sparing me from watching her recover.

Life closed twice when my mother and father died, worlds apart but gone, and now I wasn't certain I could outlast a third event, of Laura leaving, even in the house with me but not present, always turned in, protecting herself from me.

Even if I could trick myself into counting on a miraculous machine of the gods swooping in at the last minute, I realized how risky it'd be to count on something like a wealthy benefactor to hear about my plight and sympathize when I didn't have a sports skill to get my name around or hail from an inner city successful people like to donate to in memory of their roots. You can also be musical and get supported, but the farthest I'd gotten toward developing my talent was thinking about taking piano lessons from the preacher's wife, so I wasn't involved in anything that'd make somebody like Stevie Wonder or Sammy Davis Jr. take notice.

Then I'd think, How would they even hear about you on your road? Talent scouts don't tend to blow through here. There wasn't an uncle in the television industry who could get Walter Cronkite to inspire all his viewers to donate a dime to help pave the rest of the road to the future.

A couple of weeks later, on the morning this present school year started, I was standing on the edge of the road, looking back at the square hedge bushes and the clean brick steps Laura and I had sat on after supper so often that summer, still seeing the vision I'd created of the dump truck sent with best regards by the gang at CBS World News, to pour a silver stream of dimes into a massive mound in the yard.

The bus arrived and the doors opened and I got on and said hey to people I felt like I hadn't seen in a year although I just saw them yesterday at the store or downtown Saturday buying new clothes. As we lost sight of my house, I knew Laura was about to take her bath and listen to the morning shows through the open bathroom door. She could relax well with nothing to resent. I couldn't put her out by leaving her. Whatever I did about leaving, I'd have to accomplish through realism, and beyond Laura and the people on the bus I loved, I didn't trust much. More than anything, I trusted myself to work and knew what I felt about the kind of individuals who mash the snooze button on the clock and stay there, continuing to roll and wallow.

Once I began taking on jobs and studying like a fiend, I got a sideline benefit. Working constantly up to the utmost possible edge of sleeping kept the space my mother had left more filled. If leisure wasn't well-planned, worry over where she was now would move into the time like a bumptious stranger and addle me out of a place in line. That sliver between wakefulness and sleeping was particularly hazardous if I left what happened inside it to chance. All hell could break loose, and I loathed feeling forced to search for my mother in the flames and listen for her in the screaming of everyone her funeral preacher had said was confined to torment by an outraged God who didn't need or want help carrying out His will. Sometimes, I used the time to think of ways she could've been spared. Random as science was, there was more justice in the laws of nature, more mercy, well-deserved, than in rules that said her decision to die was unforgivable. Whoever could claim that she had enough gall to throw God's gift back in His face didn't know her very well, but unless she'd been allowed to get in on the tickets they give to people like pygmies and life-long coma victims who have never been exposed to religion. If I believed the rules, I had to believe they applied to her, so I took a personal doubt holiday that will last until undeserved cruelty, then, now, and thereafter, seems acceptable.

The only road to silent peace was through the words I wrote down to keep, more for the sounds than the meanings, that were always able to carry me to where I was able to rest, holding back the old sounds and scenes that have had time to organize themselves inside me and grow as strong as men, so you learn by heart and you're grateful to say,

> Philanthropist, opulent, honorific, keening,
> Tumult, tumultuous, compatible, breast-feeding,
> Cinema, efficient, evermore, cellar door,
> For I have eaten ashes like bread and mingled my
>   drink with weeping,
> That I may learn in my own life and away from home
>   and friends
> What the heart is and what it feels.
> Beadsman, celibate, cenobite, friar,
> Mendicant, palmer, pilgrim, prior.
> Mother of God, Amen, Mother of God, so be it.

Three

LOOK AROUND MY HOUSE AND SEE WHY THE BEAUTY here knocks me off my feet every few minutes of the day. There's a kind of love behind the thoughtfulness you see when you open the door to a room that draws you inside to sit down and gaze, enjoying how welcomed you feel and trusted as well not to spoil things. How many times have you been in a place where the lady of the house is so wadded up by fear of spilling on the sofa she's kept it enclosed in plastic, and how many people have you visited who lacked the edge of sophistication to realize that they were supposed to unwrap the lampshades once they got them back to their living rooms from the display living rooms at Sears? You see Laura's confident tastes and her refusal to let life revolve around terror of stains impressing visitors when they come in, and even though other women on our road may not be able to go through with finally stripping their plastic when they leave here, they behave like it's the amazement it is that she can interior decorate like out of a magazine and mix tones of paint in brave and unique ways without anything about herself or her house making them feel like lesser housekeepers or victims of families that wouldn't appreciate anything new they might try.

Martha's mother visits when the store is closed of a Sunday afternoon and takes a nap in the guest room, generally without letting her family know where she is. If you saw the wreckage from Martha's five brothers in the house, you'd know why she parks where you can't see her car driving by and refuges in what she calls the peace of mind room down here. Before I saw it clearly, Laura explained her resting as she was making her a pot of tea to wake up with, saying, Women hide women, Ellen. Sometimes you have to make one wash her hair and go downtown, and sometimes you have to help one have a little rest and rustication from her life. And don't tell Martha her mother's here when she's missing. It's only two or three hours, but the child will decide she's poisoned and want to nag her mother for the antidote.

I said, But if Martha or her brothers have an accident or something, and they can't find their mother, what about an emergency like that?

You see it, she said, through your eyes, but the reality is there's another able adult in the house, asleep in front of a football game, and that's the only time he's in the house all week, so he can learn to be on his feet and alert if his children need him.

I didn't need to ask Laura whether she needed to be hidden from me. I followed her down the hall with the tin of mail order shortbread she allowances out for visitors.

You open the door to the guest bedroom that used to be the scrambled, moxed mess the other two foster girls lived in and see the fabric coordinated, not matching but still good, on the padded window seat, the bed, and the straight, long-hanging curtains. Stay here a while and learn that a suit of clothes drapes on your body, drape is a verb, not a noun, and you wash your hands in the sink, not the zinc, which is not to say my way of speaking was oafish before I got here. My mother's history had her say, like Laura, stockings instead of hose, undergarments for bloomers, drawers, panty leggings, and step-ins, and if we'd had more than a few belongings in our house, they would've been arranged in this appropriate way, like a cottage motel royalty would say they found agreeable to stay in. I had to move a silver rose bowl, for example, to put the tea tray down, and when I set it on the dresser, I had to move aside a dozen or so kooky windup tin toys we keep there for Starletta to stay occupied with when she comes over.

Taking a look around the living room, there's a wooden bowl of many woods on the mantel and two pewter candlesticks at each end, and hanging over it is an old window we made into a picture frame, and where the windowlights should be are scenes of us on various holidays and one of Starletta and me dressed out as macaroni and cheese on the first Halloween I was here. On the round cherry table nearby is a tall lamp and a slender, floral painted shade and a golden frame with a picture of me fishing Starletta out of the bobbing for apples barrel that same year. Laura's theory is you keep the public surfaces free of everything except for a lamp, a book, and a thing, so the end tables by the sofa have a lamp, a box we keep arrowheads in, and books you think are important for people to pick up and leisurely read in: We Are Your

Sons, about Julius and Ethel Rosenberg and how their sons fiercely believe they weren't criminals, a biography of Franklin and Eleanor Roosevelt, and a book of T. S. Eliot poems called Four Quartets, which helped when some Jehovah's Witnesses dropped by and didn't want to understand that a poet could work religion into his themes.

One thing to note is watch out when you sit on the large leather ottoman over near the kitchen. If the hidden wheels aren't braced, it'll slide out from under you, or if you hold on and push against the sofa, you can jump the threshold and ride past the appliances and the sink, usually ending up in the area in front of the back door, where you clean dirt off your feet. It's not a room specifically though it goes by the name mudroom. I haven't ridden the stool since I moved in, but since we changed out the kitchen linoleum for hard tile, there isn't a problem with pushing Starletta. Laura dreads Stuart wanting to take off on it, banging dents, but it has to do with his size and how he doesn't realize the force of his own weight, so as long as you're not that heavy and know to do it once and then stop, she'd say go ahead. All she asks is you not behave like you were raised in a floored pen, which isn't a problem for people who quickly pick up on the news that things are a rung or two above the typical, tear-it-up wrestling den. There's no wooden fork and spoon on the wall, no easy recliner, the pale yellow quilted satin she sewed lays across the arm of the sofa, not across the back, like in an invalid house, nothing sateen or shag, no burnt orange or vanilla incense, no sign saying to Bless This Mess and no mess.

Laura despises filth and chaos and believes there's self-respect in getting up and doing what calls for bleaching first, and since the other two girls left, she hasn't had to endure anybody struggling against the order here, which is not to name me perfection, but glancing slights like faking sleep when I don't want to delve into the day or shifting when she reaches to touch me because of something like a bad monthly mood that takes things beyond your ability to be caressing are nothing in comparison to how the other girls treated her. If you don't want to sleep for a few days, go into her room after she's slowly closed herself up in there to sit on the edge of her bed a few minutes and recover from some ugly choice you made to be stubborn. Apologize and hear it's fine or she needs time because of a remark you made about how you'd put out a leg and thumb to Baltimore before you'd accept a charity dime for the train fare, and then go back and ball yourself up in the nice chair she bought you and regard the words that come out of your mouth and cringe at what a big shot you sounded like. Make a mistake with your mouth in this beautiful place with the woman who rescued you from the fate of strangers and uncaring aunts, and see how much power you have and how dangerous and easy it is to slip into being the kind of girl who damages women. Then total how far a distance there is between you right then and women who love enough to keep a friend hidden of a Sunday afternoon and waken them with English tea in a china pot and a tin of biscuit treats they can't have at home because everything gets consumed out from under them.

You hope it's only human nature that makes you uncivilized around the edges sometimes, and you tell yourself you aren't like the others who took too much. Compare and contrast the freedom you feel to breathe freely and go in and out of the rooms without worrying about opening a door to their rough company on the other side. In the girls' bedroom I would hear males being big shots, talking about their deals like somebody sixteen has business enterprises, ripping into the Little Debbie cakes I took for lunch and leaving the box gaped empty in the pantry, flagrant about behaving like they owned the place when Laura wasn't here and crawling in the windows when she was. She eventually found them out by following a trail of sorriness, and one evening when she came in from the movies early and cleaned her way to them, stooped over with their floor trash in her hands and opened the door on their party, the clash and conflict I'd expected didn't happen.

She said, If you don't live here, get out, and you two, sit here until I can speak. I'm going to think. Then I'll speak.

I heard her on the phone to Starletta's mother, saying the girls were growing up downhill and she was afraid, she said, on account of the quality and quantity of attention they were after. I thought she'd say I was a relief or my problems were at least not proning me toward sexuality diseases, but she didn't, and although the girls tried to move the topic off them and onto things like how unhealthy it was for me to read all night and how I existed to turn them in for minor trivialities, she wouldn't be varied off them. She taped rules on the refrigerator, which I thought gave out too much world to operate in, especially for the busty one with the new driving license, but they only felt more fenced in. They tore beyond the outline and pressed in all directions while I watched what I'd come here for become completely disdone.

The minute Laura cranked the car to be gone more than an hour, they were phoning up characters to come over, common, hostile old friends and relations in the main from their old lives, untrustworthy people. They sniffed around Laura's bedroom belongings and stole her sample bottle of Chanel Number 5, leaving her to think it'd fallen off her dressing table into the trash I'd then carried out and disposed of. I had to stand between two strumpets and a woman disappointed over her only perfume, wondering if family loyalty to girls with evil gene pools and hordes of imprisoned people in their genealogy meant keeping the truth in until my lips exploded. You wondered if she'd say I shouldn't have told her because family members have permission to be treacherous and protect one another, but I wasn't aware of that because instructions on everyday life in the family unit weren't installed in me young.

I hit the limit of the rock and the hard place on a school vacation day when Laura drove Starletta's mother and her to the teaching hospital to meet a new doctor. When she said she'd be gone from dawn to dusk, you could see the wheels turning with the girls' plans on the good time that was due to be had by all. They kept enticing me to visit people, but I said I'd rather stay in my room, which they took as a sign I'd be lurking and phoned people up saying Old Ellen might find herself on the far side of a locked door and so on. Laura hated to trust them, but they said they recognized she had the one nerve left, and if they danced on it, that would be that. Earlier than they usually managed to wake up for school, they were sneaking their favorite gang of foulmouth grabbers in, including a boy who bragged he was AWOL and several who looked like they'd be diseased down there. Then I heard the clothes dryer buzzer go off over the record player and racket, and when I opened the laundry room, I knocked into the army criminal and a girl with face skin that looked like potato chips participating in something so far toward sex you could call it sex.

They created scenes of chaos they couldn't put back in order fast enough. When Laura came home early and walked into this one, she went to her bed and cried, mainly, she said, because she hadn't left them in the middle of the night, this had been a weekday morning, which made her feel like something not quite violent but definitely unfriendly had jumped out at her, stubborn deaf and blind to the day she'd spent doing a good thing. The hours bundled into stacks of days she'd spent on them that were now looking like futile time she could've used elsewhere. When they all finally left, including the girls, I said, If I was you, I'd call the veteran and have him change the locks and stand in here and turn some tough love on them when they set up banging to get in.

She said, I know, and it's sad, this route they've taken, but the families they come from are sadder, and it's only a couple of months until things at home are straight enough for them to be back there. So maybe let's try to be patient. Maybe you could stay overnight at a friend's if things aren't comfortable here.

I said, I don't mean to say it's turned upside down, but I don't know if the one behaving ought to be the one put out. This wasn't part of the program when I said I wanted to be here permanently.

Not put out, she said, just a couple of nights, if they do something like this again.

I said, But why can't they just be decent instead of me having to pack another suitcase? Part of what I was given was a fair amount of patience, but those girls expect to keep draining the well continuously. My family may not be in jail, but they're still either dead or crazy, and I'm the one here losing sleep over taking a sliver of pie.

You can't make people behave, she said, by force of will, and you should try harder not to panic when things feel a little out of place.

I said, It's the middle of the day and somebody's crying in the house. What if one of them gets a baby in here? Suppose they drag people in that hurt us, not our perfume, but us bodily? And they're not upset right now. They're at Wright's Chick Shack, laughing about us in the parking lot. It seems to be very relaxing not to have anything expected of you, but I'm worn out watching it. I thought it'd be peace for more than a few minutes.

Yes, she said, I know you did, and when I can think about what to do about them, I'll do it, but you may just have to be patient. There aren't many people who'll take older girls, even briefly.

Because we cause so much commotion, I told her. That's what people think.

She said, You know you don't.

I said, No, it's okay. Then I left the house and rode my bicycle down to Martha's store and used the pay phone to call the foster office and say I was sorry to report it, but I knew of some girls the foster office needed to come on back out here and load up because through no fault of their new mother's and the hoopla they'd created on their own, they were bordering on being out of hand, and if anyone needed evidence, they could be found drinking alcohol out of sacks outside a take-your-clothes-off place in town, where one or the both of them was nursing an ambition to work. When the lady asked where Laura was all this time, I said, Same place as she always is, at home and hearth, doing the very best she can.

Laura was supposed to be told only so much of what I'd said, but riding back home, as my forearms began to numb and hot stomach acids began to attack, I realized you can't trust the government after Watergate. Riding to my house felt so much like riding to my doom that I sat on the steps when I got there, hoping she'd be worried enough around dark to speak to me in relief rather than with a sting in her voice. If I hadn't been worried about being seen by somebody riding by, one plan was to turn the bicycle over in the ditch and have it lay there on top of my body a while, anything not to hear her say I'd destroyed two girls to save myself, and I'd never be the kind of woman who shelters a friend if I was this conniving about putting them back in their pasts before people there were wholly healed and ready for them.

The crunch of the granite rocks in the driveway is
generally loud, particularly if the bicycle tires need air in
them, but when I rode up, it sounded like I was grinding
them between my ears. I knew she heard me because the
front curtains parted, and when the door opened, I exploded into a wild kind of weeping just as she said, Well,
just sit here and get pulled together because you want to
be in fairly good shape when they show up for this emergency investigation, or they may take you, too, take you,
take me, take them, close the house down, Ellen, and take
us all. You see, you said the girls were out of control, so
it naturally follows that I'm allowing them to run wild
and leave the windows cracked for the boys and get by
with all these other offenses you must've done an excellent job listing.

Mother of God, I said, they're after you? Are they
taking me?

Ten or fifteen years from now, she said, I'm sure it'll
be hilarious, but right now it's not. You described this as
a mess of an ordinary day.

I said, I was trying to fix it.

Patience, you needed to manage for another few
weeks. I told you.

But, I told her, it sounds like a long time. It's been so

little of life, you know what I mean to say, right, and now they'll end it again?

She pushed the ottoman over and sat down with her knees jabbed up to mine and told me, Your life, your life isn't the only one here.

But I was making something of it, I told her. They were just treating their life like a motel, you know, not attached, and I've been making things.

Yes, she said, you have, and they've been alive and doing fairly what they've known how to do at the time.

Martha's oldest brother had told me about seeing them in unsightly places in town, and I had a sudden picture of them going through a siren arrest and having my name on their lips while their mug shots were taken. I said, Maybe they weren't that bad. I guess I can take it. Let me call the foster office and say I lost my head and passed some false rumors or something and you were upset over something else I didn't know about yet.

So instead of us sounding like two extremely mean-spirited and disturbed people, we'll sound like Lucy and Ethel, she told me. If I were you, I'd dry my face and get back to whatever I was doing, and don't phone up anybody else, either here or behind the meat counter down at Martha's place. Let me get dinner together and let me manage this, and Ellen, think before you do this the next time, think a thing completely through.

I did, I said.

When? On your way down there?

I said, I've thought about what to do once I started living all my life, and I thought this was how you did it. I don't need supper though. Martha made ham sandwiches while I was on the telephone.

When I got to my room, I couldn't rest, so I wrote some on how things had corroded so darkly from where the girls had been the first day I saw them with Laura with a kind of bright light of bliss around them and thought they were set to live out the orphan American dream. I stayed out of my skin, thinking about how to be a part of this group that seemed to take for obvious granted that you change your underwear daily and hand-wash your brassiere in Ivory Snow once a week, and when the moment came for me to find a place to live again, even though there's only the one road everything in my life has always operated off of, all the roads led to here.

The roads would come together here and conclude. I'd move elsewhere for college eventually and do the epidemic disease research and come home for holidays bringing Laura unique presents from across the international date line. If she wanted to, she could come with me a few times, the way Starletta's probably going to do. This was the story I'd started writing here, and when it was snatched by people who interrupted with jangling, ill-fitting contributions, I couldn't throw up my hands and let the work and words scatter like October leaves on me. If you want a rhythm in your life as dependable as the seasons, you can allow only so much outlandish weather in before things become too confused to repair.

I was finishing the picture of me staggering up out of the ditch, miraculously clean when Laura came in, saying summarized, Don't trust that anything you mox in again like this is going to work out according to your specifications, and believe me, your life is going to be enough to keep up with from now on.

What happened was I landed on my feet because the girls were more or less off theirs by the time the lady got someone downtown to find them. Laura helped place them with married gym teachers she knew who had a knack for converting the wild, and by the time their families were ready for them, I heard they were routine girls who merely lived in town and reported to school and their part-time jobs on time.

I told Laura, It sounds like the girls probably slowed down out of a lack of somebody to get a charge out of and simple boredom.

Good, she said. There's a great deal to be said for boredom, not all of it bad. It leads to naps, although I know it'll be a while before I find you asleep during the day without sitting down to feel you for fever. It's you here now and the company we have wishes you well, so there's nothing stopping you from saying there's nothing to do so you're going to take your shoes off and get on top of the covers with your clothes on. You've learned to love and work well enough without a guidebook, and since I'm supposed to have one for you, I can tell you the next chapter's on rest though if you need a higher authority, I understand that citizens of Spain and France and I don't know where else are expected to rest, more than a little siesta. The idea of rest equals the idea of work, and I think they smear love throughout automatically, and I see another automatic thing, odd but nice, I think. Other people notice it to me, but I'm just hearing it. I sound like you, I hear old Ellen in me. Do you hear it? Listen to us, amazing.

Four

WATCH ME WALK, I CARRY MY HANDS TO THE sides. I don't lurch or slope. There's not a hunchback dome on my back. I can walk rested in the shoulders and loose armed, or I can walk with dignity, like a queen. After three years here, it's only loose ends left to manage, but when the list of things you have left to do on yourself includes items such as healing from terror that comes and goes and frequently gets in your way, it looks like the large job of work it still is. The good news was I was on the brink of October.

If you think about October's role in the calendar, you'll see it was custom-created to relieve the sensation of unsettledness and the mingling fears and needs that still edged in if I took a brief vacation, and let my mentalities go lax the way people my age who don't have to feel old as vampires have the privilege to do. October promises a difference and brings it, the changes it says are coming always come. When the air crispens, it splurges on symbols, dropping beautiful proof at your feet. It doesn't lie or leave out, saying death will be around eventually but only because life was already here, and here's some color and snappy weather and flocks of birds flying south to allow you to breathe deeply in trust that the universe knows what to do and when to do it. There won't be haywire shocks to wound the sky and shatter down another dose of jagged edges. October knows you've had enough.

The rhythm of the world out here picks up when the farmer across the road begins plowing after he's brought in his main crops and sold them so he can settle his affairs at Martha's family's store and with the man who delivers his fuel oil. On he'll go around to businesses until everybody who helped him during the past year has been paid. Crossing the wide ditch and walking behind him as the ground's being turned over to expose arrowheads, which you may find one or several of, I was getting dirty in the good clothes I shouldn't have been over there in. When he gave me a couple of flints he'd found earlier, he didn't notice it to me or say he'd heard I wanted to go to college early, and I knew he had, he's Stuart's uncle. He talked about what he talks about, asking how one of his elderly ex-teachers is faring and whether I'm still passing my hard lessons in school.

After he's plowed the last row, he plants pumpkins to replace needed nutrients harsher crops like to strip up, and they grow so hurriedly that you look out the window again and he's over there, laying by. Look again and he's walking around, admiring them. By the middle of October, you can tell he's settled his bills not just by his improved posture but by how he's changed the sweat-banded cap he wore all summer to a Frank Sinatra hat he got out shopping with his family last Saturday. He's in a good mood because anybody is who's just been to Sears. I knew Stuart had also been there the second I walked down the aisle of the bus and tripped across his new Wolverines.

The people I go around with have never been model students, but October uplifts the least likely to read on his own and those with the worst collections of checkered report cards. Instead of getting to school and closing everything up in their lockers to droop around the rest of the day empty-handed, you'll see them thinking about the right books to take out. Stuart doesn't usually carry anything in his hands besides leftovers from our table's lunches and a black film between his fingers, but every October he comes in with a box of decorative gourds he brings for his teachers to think back on when they grade him.

He trogged past my locker, where some people were standing around with Starletta demonstrating the lit-up seasonal pin her mother varies on her dress collar. He stopped and said, Huh, a pumpkin? I thought it would've been a scarecrow pin. Huh, I aint studying pumpkins. Aren't they squash?

Luther said, I don't know, does it matter?

He turned back to Starletta, who's twelve now, with the body of a six-year-old and the mind of a friendly older toddler. Although she goes around oblivious, she's stuck beside me through thick and thin. Everybody knows her and loves having her around. She's the kind of famous person that if you don't know her, you know of her, and information like how she follows behind Luther a great deal and wears the changing seasonal light-up pins on her collar, though to me she's most known for her joy and gorgeous soul.

You want Luther to look like Marlon Brando but he doesn't. He lives on the other side of the pasture and has a semi-domesticated bobcat in his front yard. Setting the box down and wiping all over and around on top of his head with his arm, Stuart said, Only thing I know is I aint studying these vegetables. Swear before God my feet hurt, blisters, it's the Wolves. Mama said to treat them with lard, but huh, I guess I didn't.

Then you'll have to hobble, I told him, come on.

He knew I meant it was time for us to go out and sit on the low rock wall in front of the school. You could spend homeroom there if your class was on that side of the building and the teacher was willing to yell the roll out the window. Then everybody goes to their rooms and I'd recluse with Mrs. Delacroix and the books Johns Hopkins told me to have read in two weeks, which Stuart saw while we were on the wall outside. While he was repeating himself on what I was doing with a stack of new, thick books, where I was going and why, how I was getting there, when I'd be back, Marvin, Luther's first cousin, spoke over him to ask if I'd look over some poems he'd been assigned to compose. Then he got up to show them to me. Stuart didn't stop talking, he stared off and went on with the questions. With Starletta beside him, fixated on pulling the stem over and over to light up her pin, they made a world of a pair.

When Marvin brought me his opened notebook all the pages that should've had writing on them had it, there were no blank pages after doodles of guns and cars covering the first few. That had to be October's enthusiasm. Martha walked up late while I was trying to understand what his assignment had been. She'd had to open the store, so we all said, Huh, with Stuart and went back to what we were doing, except for Luther who jumped up and straddled the ditch for her to adore him doing.

Stop or fall in, Martha told him. Boy howdy, Luther, I'm a big fan of you stretched across a drainage ditch. Heave Stuart up and throw him. Throw his box of squash. They're heavy, that'd be sexy to me, wouldn't it, wouldn't it, huh, huh. Thawing the fish locker this morning was a better use of my time.

He straddled and she hounded him while Marvin kept on, She could of said do rhyming, or not, I forgot to copy the board down. I wisht I'd get a A on it though, got a F now, didn't turn in much when school started. Mumber how hot it was? Me and deddy like to of had to sleep in the chimley. Know how cool brick is?

He lives with his father in a very tiny house built close to the river, not like the holiday homes with the overhanging deck, but as in erosion. Laura trades turns with women who take them casserole dishes, and it's getting so steadily worse that by Christmas, water will flow through the door when they open it, given the sharp angled dip. I was in the library when the Earth Science class covered erosion and used his house as a kind of object lesson since everybody in there had either been to it or heard about it. He and his father probably had enough sturdy wood left for a lean-to, but he never mentioned an upcoming move or condemnation notice, and his school supplies were in excellent shape, so maybe if he had a dry place to study and sleep in, he felt fine. But I wasn't sure he would've seemed shaken if his house had took off drifting because of the way his basic nature and a life of hunting their non-casserole meals made his movements slowly careful.

I moved from wondering how he'd kept his homework clean to what he wanted me to fix. He said, I bet I'll get a A if you rhymed it, give you a dollar to do it.

The poem he'd written seemed meant to be shouted, and I'd need to turn the volume down on it first, but when I said for him to keep the dollar he was taking out of his pocket, Martha said, You phone me up, whining about the load these extra schools could put on Laura and how much Harvard costs, then turn a dollar down. Come get on at the store and have my mother tell you being lucky there's a store to work in is wages enough. You probably need, what, nine hundred thousand more of them? I wouldn't turn my nose up at one.

So I took the dollar, but for reasons I couldn't fathom, Luther took a B-plus on,

The First Day of Hunting Season

On the first day of hunting season,
You don't need another reason,
To rise early like the same bird,
You'll shoot from the sky, take my word.

The woods aren't dark and deep,
There's undergrowth and scrub by your feet,
But hunting's still the fall experience,
That keeps you feeling delirious.

Even in the winter gloom,
When you don't want to leave your room,
You have meat in the locker and maybe a pelt,
To help you remember how hunting season felt.

While he copied the poem in his writing, Stuart said, I wish you wouldn't talk to people when I want to say something to you, huh. I dislike them breaking in.

Nerves had beaded sweat on his head, which he soaked up by pressing both jacket sleeves in over his ears. I said, Are you going to do your head or tell me what the matter is?

Nothing, he said, I just dislike it is all, but, huh, you still didn't tell me why you brought all these books that don't belong with you. I wish you'd say something on it before school takes in.

What hair he had was a light orange-tinged yellow, but despite the sweat, he wasn't carrying the odor you'd expect because of how October also brought personal hygiene benefits, coming between the Indian summer heat and the winter plague of cloakroom lice. Knowing words, sweat, and tears would start pouring, I didn't want to tell him about Baltimore, but he could also make a day long, so I told it rapidly and left to take Starletta to her room when the first names were yelled out for the roll. I'd be under the compulsion to go to his house after school, where he'd be sitting on a bucket and poking a long stick at his family's continually burning rubber pile.

He sounds broke but you'd be surprised at how many times you'll be with his family and see them take out twenty-dollar bills to pay for things. It's very profitable for his father to drive up and down the interstate highways, relieving truck stops and service stations of shot tires he brings home and adds to the rubber pile, which is almost taller than the house, continuously smoking but not flaming. You'd think a man who does that would be putting his family in the strait of siphoning gas from the lawn mower to the car or taking twenty-three coupons to Martha's store to exchange for a penny and starting a fight over exactly what the fine print says the cash value is, things the family out here that eats off records does when nobody's needing any of the secondhand merchandise the father sets around in their yard. The first time I heard Laura use a vocabulary word was when she used lucrative, as in, I had no idea that trading in used rubber could be lucrative enough to keep Stuart's mother in Cadillacs. I'm stunned.

Since I've lived closer to this end of the road and

nearer to Stuart than I did when we were little, I'm on a bucket beside him by the rubber pile fairly often. I wouldn't want it to sound like it's exploded more than once, and then only because of the gasoline and matches he threw on it last summer to protest his father leaving him there to nurse his mother through the insanity and hard recovery she suffered after her hysterectomy. Except for then, I haven't seen it flame, so I don't waste time picturing Salem executions there. You couldn't call it a pyre, but it's technically interesting because of the absence of odor, like Stuart's sweat, nobody smells it.

We could've adapted, but you wouldn't know unless you flagged down some strangers and asked them to stick their head out the window in the vicinity of Stuart's house and say whether they smell toxic fumes or smoke and supper rising from Starletta's house. That's mainly all we smell out here since Starletta's father died and her mama started soaking up the spare hours by volunteer cooking for the shut-in delivery program at some churches I helped her clean to raise educational money. The theory is the stranger would say, Smoke and supper, and go on. Stuart's mother is at ground zero and didn't birth maldeformed children. Even if we were to learn enough about toxic waste to believe different, I couldn't call the government and say I was reporting my neighbors for burning a dangerous hole in the sky.

Maybe I'd procrastinated on living in October the way I wanted to because it was hard to believe there could be pleasure in anything I hadn't earned. Maybe rotating around from a temporary state of the blues to the magic of all being well and perfectly fine became too much of a sure custom, like Starletta's pins. The prizes for talent and striving and the adaptation skills I'd used to get them would feel thrilling for a while, and work and words would keep my mother's empty space filled, but then everything would open again, more infinite ended, and I'd wonder if other individuals were rolling into the future this way and what they did to correct it.

I stayed at it, filling and carrying on a constant discussion with myself about how to live in a place that seemed endless and bottomless, studying nonchalant people who manage to cross streets, open doors, drink from water fountains, or tie their shoes without needing to scream about how banty-weighted and trifling they feel in this large, loud cave they've been forced to go around inside. The nothing now where my mother had been could shock repeatedly, the way a forgetful baby can get blown down when he touches the same ragged light cord each time he crawls by it.

When the door opened now, my mother wasn't the one coming in with groceries and noticing I'd remembered to thaw out the chicken and soak it in milk. She wasn't the one beside me at the Elizabeth Arden counter the day it opened, enticing me to try a little color on my cheeks, nothing heavy, something sheer. Laura was the wrong person doing the right things, and even on days when I almost forgot and it barely mattered that her hair was thick, black, and long, rather than short in brown waves, that she was strong-boned instead of frail, there was no way to forget or correct the fact that I didn't live inside my mother's mind anymore. I wasn't the first and last thought of her day. The hole was emptier than holes with merely nothing in them, it was missing everything that had been possible before. The space was sunk down inside me, like the raw, gouged place there had been in her chest, where her heart was taken out and worked on and then slipped back down and sewn into her a few weeks before the pills she swallowed made it beat so rapidly it couldn't bear the strain and finally, quietly quit.

I went around like a person wearing the wrong size shoes, willing to cut toes off or manage with some broken to keep carrying what my mother did and still walk with a posture that wouldn't draw attention. It was an odd, old show, never stopping to take the shoes off because I stayed so fixated on changing myself instead of them. You realize your method of being in the world isn't a mindless habit. You can do better, but there never seems to be the proper moment to halt everything and get the shoes off and go on forward, so you push on with working. You do not get caught being the old, odd vampire girl on your road.

You're one of those people who have to prove they deserve to be kept on at the countinghouse, and you can be too tired to think but you'll do it, do it again and keep doing what you have to do because you're also too scared of being marked off to stop. And at the end of the day, you go home with the proof of your labors, and she's glad to see someone who's always so willing to do everything precisely and create such large, perfect portions. In a universe they claim is unfolding just as it should, I believe you'll survive and be fine if you know better than to be ruthless and are ashamed to be greedy. You may not be capable of slowing down, but you can manage to look around and be grateful for the day on your rapid way through it.

Five

YOU THINK SMART MEANS WISE. THEN YOU HOPE it will soon. This past autumn, I ran along two parallel lines of wanting more ease and keeping myself endangered of strict consequences for selling poetry. After I branched out on Martha's tip and word got across to the high school as well as to the Apocalypse school, money began coming in so hand over fist that the fear of going to the poorhouse if I went to Baltimore changed into a let-them-eat-cake ease. Clothes to wear up there began flying off layaway. You merely had to take out the savings passbook on the college tuition account I halved the profit into and check the interest compounding to remember the rewards of labor and thrift.

Caught up, I ignored common sense saying to deposit less into the college fund and have more time for the camp, and when they sent a bill for what I owed after the scholarship figure was discounted out, it was either shortchange the future, borrow from Laura, or stay home. I went up there owing her two hundred dollars, a drop in the bucket on the overall costs, but enough by itself to roil through your system at night like Ebenezer's crumb of disturbing bad cheese, so I continued on with the poetry industry, at home, on the bus, on the low wall outside school, anywhere I could find to focus with the ghosts of broke pasts hovering over me.

If you felt strained by English, you could choose a precomposed poem for two dollars or get a custom-made one for four. Concrete poetry ran at least a dollar higher. Sonnets would've been five if they'd been assigned, but Mrs. Delacroix said teachers didn't because it was equal to requiring students to explain the hydrogen bomb and it wasn't worth the frustration to dwell on outsized skills at a school that excused you two days off a year to get in hay and kill hogs on your farm.

Twenty of the poems that made up a separate selection book, entitled Meditations on Life Passing You By, came in a flat rush while I was on the way to Baltimore, trying to keep everything about the trip from getting out from under me. When the train pulled away from our station, I had to crawl over a lady to wave out the window at Laura, Stuart and his mother, Starletta and her mother who'd come by to say Study hard, make friends, we'll be here when you get back. When I made it back to my seat I was too edgy to read and too knotted up to eat even a salted cracker out of my box lunch. Before I knew it, I'd started getting up and down and attracting looks to where I wanted to tell people, I'm just overwhelmed is all.

The lady looked at me like she wanted to ask me whether my mother had packed me with some kind of pill but instead she asked where I was headed, and I told her I was going to learn about how artistic things compare and contrast with science. God knows how much time I'd chewed up wondering things like how somebody first put math and moods together in iambic pentameter, the truth of van Gogh's ear issue, why so many great geniuses have bad wrecks for lives, for example, how Poe was full of a lust for life yet crippled by his appetites and jealousy.

She said, Where are you going to do that?

In Baltimore, I said, where Poe finally threw up his hands and fell, on a walking tour. Speaking of which, I wouldn't mind hitting my shoes with the polish a time or two more before we get there. I'll be right back.

I'd gone by Laura's old etiquette book for advice to young ladies traveling alone by rail because going to Baltimore on a train had a 1958 tinge to it. I'd used what Martha's twin high school brothers had paid for two themes on the meaning of I Must Go Down to the Sea Again, and the bonus for making twin work different enough for the saddle oxfords. I realized while I was breaking them in I'd need to rest my feet in my sneakers but the porter said people don't go back into their belongings once they're checked in. I was going to ask the lady if she'd ask him on my behalf and explain I wasn't planning to get in the baggage compartment and ramble, but when I got to my seat, she'd given it up to another lady she said was a friend, though they couldn't have been better strangers.

I got my satchel and purse from the overhead, saying I thought seats were assigned in first class and knowing she'd say there were a dozen more and she and her buddy had to catch up, the way things unfold like a story that wastes your time when you know the plot and symbols by rote. The porter said to take any seat available. I had a chapter left in the only book that wasn't packed in the bag he still wouldn't allow me into, so tensing over the destination, cranked up with the thrill of train travel itself, and pitched at a level the gentleman beside me behaved like he didn't want to endure. On the way back over him, I mentioned how I didn't want to end up like a friend of mine who was still nursing blisters from Wolverines and said, Wish me luck on breaking in these hard shoes.

Stuart had actually been the one to rub them with saddle oil the previous evening, but giving a sales-looking man a practical reason for my walking up and down the aisle and crossing over rattling connections seemed more likely to discourage him from giving away my seat. I said I'd be back in a minute, but I found it took a while to check out the other compartments and see what conclusions you can draw about people in different classes and what the exceptions were, like if there were wealthy people in the back class looking like they enjoyed saving money or people like me in first class who seemed to be there on a scholarship or gift. After that, I remembered I'd told Laura I'd see if the berths were like the ones in Some Like It Hot, but the woman behind the counter in the dinette car said unless you sleep reared back in your chair, this was not a sleeping train.

She kept offering me something to eat, but you hear too many stories of young people going somewhere for the first time and spending all their money on the way there. I said I didn't care for anything though her food looked good despite what I'd heard about them steaming everything by the engine. She said that was part of the legend of trains she could disprove by showing me where she took foods out of the freezer box and placed them directly into a miniature oven. Talking to someone about her job isn't chatting with the person in the other seat, so I didn't mind explaining about not wanting to arrive spent out or about the steam. When we stopped at Union Station in Washington DC, she said to come in with her while she picked up her family's pastries and have a coffee and bagel with her at a table under the dome to see what that was like. I can say now that it was supersaturating without feeling dazey again, so anyone whose legs are prone to vibrate when something like the curved top of the world is revealed, should hold the rail or sit and allow the rushers to pass.

I thought I'd talked enough to the dinette woman to be quiet when I sat down again by the man, but when you take off from the station you're blown out of a tunnel into a bright force of light, and I had to say, I apologize, but look at everything outside the window. I can't believe we're moving through it this fast, Mother of God, this is quick. It's like it's moving by you, but it's entirely the opposite and something to think about. If you don't mind me doing it, I'd like to write it down now and not wait and look back in tranquility and probably be wasteful forgetting. What do you think?

He said, I think that'd be fine. You go ahead and do that, but don't hold it against me if I go to sleep.

I told him I envy sleep actually, and when he woke up in Baltimore three hours later he said the breakdown we'd had earlier would make him late for a job meeting. I didn't want to lose the work and he wasn't in the mood or I could've torn him out a poem entitled, On the Road to Nowhere Rapidly. There were twenty-five poems, with an overall theme of carpe diem with a sideline of Beauty. Titling it Meditations on Life Passing You By came from mixing the common sense of how I was watching out the window with the symbolism of how we all should stare out less and seize so much more. Four or five poems became alike when the breakdown stalled the scenery at a very small town with a couple of stores and a few houses. I got over the hump of repeatedly writing how depressed you'd have to be living there by finally writing,

If at First You Cannot Leave

If at first you cannot leave this village of woe,
Because you are bound to your relatives,
Look outside your window and see,
The train stalled outside your small depot,
And ask yourself what's interesting about the tracks,
Sit on your low, ragged porches to think if you must,
Then hear the whistle,
I heard it,
It blows,
And see the train in the other direction, it goes,
I saw it,
It goes,
And if you ask your family what's interesting about
    that,
And they say they have no clue,
Then say your good-byes and grab your suitcase,
And walk down your weedy town hill to board,
The next train that comes by,

But don't beat yourself up, leaving your clan,
For trains that go in one direction always come in the
    other,
And will bring you home again to visit dear old
    Mother.

I'd always counted Baltimore on the Southern side, and I'd expected the other students to hail from places I was used to meeting people from. I had no clue it was going to be more toward Harvard in the habits and ways people brought with them, so there was some rolling stomach panic going on when I realized I had to have conversations with people I hadn't had time to mentally adapt myself to yet. You don't hear how ignorant your accent makes you sound until you have to hear it against other accents, especially when you're competing with people with the edge of the accent that makes them seem like automatic experts.

I decided the trick was to hush entirely or just avoid saying anything they could doubt, but I turned from being more or less confident to thoroughly flabbergasted when I got to the check-in area where chaperones introduce students around, and a clot I had to stand in wanted to know what it was like being a curiosity in a world of nonreaders and racists. I had to leave before the panic began leaking out in balls of forehead sweat or heavy breathing. I knew the truth about where I lived and also how whipped you feel after you try to explain something to people who don't want to change their minds and would never understand how they could be the ignorant ones.

Johns Hopkins had the green quad, the archways, and a mix of modern and stone buildings, and when I followed the map to the dormitory and saw it was not only stone but many gabled, being stunned that I was spending the night in a building like this made it absolutely not matter that the people who'd just behaved like I was lost on the way to mop something up were going to be sleeping in there with me. The way the gables spiked in the sky and how you could imagine finding somebody up there in a dormer room, hunched over with a blanket around his shoulders, possibly coughing with tuberculosis, writing with papers strung and strewed everywhere, I didn't care if they believed their fate included high matters of serious beauty and mine was to ask them whether they had any more silver I need to polish.

I noticed a thin girl with red hair and slippery white skin at the top of the steps, looking at name tags as girls went by her, and then as I passed her, she said, Stop, you're my roommate. I need you to let me in to get my stuff out.

It was addling, but I understood how she so much hadn't wanted to stay with a stranger that she was willing to sleep on the floor in the room with a girl she knew from home. I thought it was also grounds to try to get along, but once we were in the room, she was out so fast that I'm not sure if her name was Lola or Nola. I just thought, Well, more power to you and arranged my things around and studied through all the assignments we'd been sent for the weekend. I was glad to be around people who took the same thing that interested me seriously. But when classes started they looked set on not finding any pleasure in it, jumping on you the second you answered a question. For instance, when I said Hemingway's stories are an example of where a writer uses a kind of science of reason to keep the emotions from getting out of hand, a long-legged boy in a sweater vest across from me at the table appeared to have no clue that you shouldn't ask a stranger, especially a female, why she didn't see the difference between reason and brain-damaged writing.

I said, I don't know. Nobody's ever asked me that kind of question. I can't answer it.

The teacher let the boy ask me why, and I said, Because of the way it was put to me.

I fumed through that class and a couple more and finally got to a class I'd been looking forward to that was held walking around in a gallery of photographs of outstanding scenery from the meatpacking plant days of Chicago and the violent early days of trade unions marching in the streets. It occurred to me to ask a teacher, being careful to do it on the side, if people being able to take pictures more conveniently was connected to people starting to write realistically. While I was walking to the library and feeling a great deal of adrenaline over things the teacher had said I should look up about Theodore Dreiser and John Steinbeck, a girl I hadn't noticed overhearing us came up beside me and said, I'm so tired of Sister Carrie I'd puke if I had to read it again.

I told her my teachers at home hadn't assigned the book yet, knowing it sounded like I went to school in a floored pen, and while I was trying to think of what they could've been preoccupied for us to study instead, she told me she was homeschooled and her mother doted on particular periods and ignored others and it grated on her.

For mercy, she trotted, I imagined, to find somebody else to expose how much she knew to, which was such a running motive there and such a blaring one that any leftover nerves I'd had about Dr. Bok thinking I was a journey-proud brag became concern the letter was too timid and so quiet that it was for all intents and purposes Braille. Being the real thing, I thought, made you confident to say less than you know and not lord information, the kind of hard moral plateaus you shoot for and may sometimes miss. Outside a couple of severe introverts, what I saw said college could be full of characters like the ones who'd crawled in the windows and blistered the calm of Laura's house, only this crowd got a sad charge out of narrating tours of the intellect and museums you hadn't been on and letting you know you weren't the first one to discover something. It didn't matter if a thousand scholars studied how Madame Bovary probably wouldn't have had to rot from the inside if she'd read better books in her girlhood, if the idea strikes you in Baltimore in a room full of people who say they already know, my theory is it's still your personal news.

By the time the librarian worked down the row to me, I didn't need her to explain their card catalog as much as I had to know where they kept the world atlases. She brought an outsized one to a table, and then I pressed my finger down on Baltimore and moved it down, thinking, I'm here, and I want to be there. When I'm there, I'll want to be here again. I was standing by a map of the world in a city I'd never been to, and neither mother could see me, and after I measured from here to there with my fingers, I moved them around west to east, and the distance put me in the middle of the ocean and proved how far out of someone's reach you could get, being pulled backward and pushed forward. Of all the things I'd learned and despite a knack for rapid imagining, I didn't know how to feel at home out in the world or at home either, though all I could think to do next was close the book and wait for a train pointed toward there.

Six

IT TOOK LUTHER AND HIS LONG-LIPPED COUSIN TO
show me the price of what had flown out of the window I'd meditated from. Our bus picked up the cousin
from the side of the road and waited while the males
pushed his car into a field. When they got back on, the
topic moved from what had just blown up under his hood
to how his clubs, the Future Farmers of America and the
Junior National Rifle Association, were teaming up to
kill enough hogs to finance an overnight excursion to the
Outer Banks for the Future Homemakers of America
club his sisters were in. Stuart was talking into my ear,
but I told him I needed to listen to how these girls were

going to see the play The Lost Colony, an outdoor drama about the settlers who became lost trying to establish a colony under grim circumstances, with the spotlight on Virginia Dare, the first little white girl born in the New World.

Laura and I had been planning to go for a while, and when I leaned up and asked Luther and his cousin whether it'd be possible for me to pay and swing a ride, Luther said, She's the girl I told you about. Tell her what English you have due Monday.

I hadn't noticed his facial features because his back had been to me, but when he turned around with his as-signment, I told him I'd look at it and barely held back asking why he'd hacked off his bangs to where they couldn't lay flat but had to dart outward from his head. It was the haircut you most associate with backwoods in-dividuals, no one very bright, but he was organizing the charity donation for the club, so maybe his mother grabbed him with the scissors, very mad, and probably disgusted with his habit of pulling his bottom lip too far out and speaking with the inner-tissue moistness exposed.

Stuart whispered in my hair, Good God, I wish he'd stop. Huh, I'd charge double to have to look at that and write.

He could've been training his lip to have a tribal plate installed, and when he offered to pick up his work, I gave back the assignment, not wanting to spend Saturday dreading Sunday. Luther spoke low and extreme, I told him you keep a stock with you usually, Ellen. You couldn't allowance him out one and do me a favor for him?

He has rhyming couplets due Monday, I told him, on nature, and I don't have any, and the weekend's already pushed, but anybody who can put together a way to get future housewives to a drama should be able to knock it out.

The cousin looked over his shoulder, saying, Never mind. I can draw one off the English book.

I said, Do what?

Draw, he said, out of the book.

When I asked if he'd ever turned in work he'd copied from his own book, he said, Not yet, hadn't had to turn in.

He had the driver let him off at the bottom of his path, and the summary of what Luther said was his cousin didn't understand that the poems in his English book or anywhere else belonged to the people who wrote them, and if they could be recited, he didn't see why he couldn't claim one. Luther couldn't say how he'd gotten to high school, never having turned in a piece of creative work, but he seemed unlikely to stay, and his mother had asked Luther to lend a hand after his improved attitude and attendance had become the talk of their family.

Luther and I got off the bus together, and standing by the ditch, looking at the large cat sleeping in his yard, he said, I tried to tell him what you said to me about this time of year being when you can pick up the beat, but his speed goes from slow to freezing if he has to write something. When he crossed the road though, the teacher said he had to start turning writing in or they'd expel him, which put his mother in a swivet, crying, calling for people to throw in and help him.

I had Luther come in the house and eat a snack or two while he waited on the arm of the chair to tell me if it favored his cousin to say,

Nature

Nature is an old wise owl,
Nature is a bobcat howl.

Nature is the only way,
Birds know where to fly and stay.

Nature's here now when it's cool,
And when you heat to death in school.

Nature is what's always around us,
Not in but outside a bus.

Nature will be on my farm of the future,
If Nature gets a grade I'm not used to.

When Luther said the poem was the image of his cousin and asked how much I wanted for it, I told him I was glad, but nothing. He said, I thought you were going to the fair tomorrow, but since you're dying, I'll tell my mother you need some soup run toward this way over the pasture.

No, I told him, not dying, not drawing poems out of a book or seized frozen either.

If I charge his cousin or anybody else for the one thing I know how to do fairly easily, I'd remind myself too much of the greedy-minded individuals from the classes, but I told Luther only, The people in Baltimore were at another extreme, and I don't see myself going there.

While you were gone, he said, Stuart told everybody you should come home on account of they had a reputation for taking legs.

His great-uncle, I said, lost his leg to diabetes in the hospital up there is all, an amputation, not body snatching.

If it was me, he said, I'd charge Stuart to take him places and be around generally. The way he's been, you wouldn't miss the profit off the poems.

I said, Tell it, and followed him to the door, watching him leave, going along through gold hay pasture. Without someone stepping in to put a frame around the view and heighten what I saw into scenery, it couldn't rise past a boy walking through a field on the side of a narrow road and be called a background. I needed to run behind him, shouting the one good, real and true thing I'd brought home from Baltimore. It felt urgent to announce how there was an individual who once loved humanity so creatively he'd called the place he'd found the Isle of Man. I also had to be struck by how the long-lengthed range of him was so giant-sized compared to the picture of him knocking his heels against a metal grammar grade desk. This tall, this rapid, the world must've been able to see us growing, moving physical upward.

When the school year started, the school nurse measured us together in her room, and there'd been the sensation of old sameness when I saw my percentile marks high on the height chart and in the low-middle on weight. Numbers didn't help me recognize myself as much as the people there with me always had. When Martha, Luther,

Stuart, and the rest went through a phase of their heads outgrowing their bodies, things were so jangled that the memory of what I saw in a mirror left when I blinked, but they reminded me that I was a girl, alive and well enough to report to school and stay available to pass through stages with other individuals.

If they smelled like the red, indented kickballs or like crayons, I knew I carried the odor of school on my hands and in my hair and liked to think it was pleasant to people, though now you'll smell Windsong on us, or Aqua Velva and our legs reach out across wide aisles and fields. They've stayed simple to be around, except for Stuart, who turned an interfering, constant longing on me about a year ago, but you behave with some honor around what can seem like foolishness, because he's a mistake waiting to happen with a heart of gold. The night before my mother's funeral, my Aunt Nadine had come and taken all my mother's things from the house, the gold compact mirror, scarves, her brush and comb, pearls, dresses, everything except a pair of stockings, which I wore rolled over and rubber-banded to school and elsewhere beyond that day until the holes were larger than my legs. The morning I returned to school after my mother's funeral, Stuart knew what I needed and gave it to me in a way I could manage. When I reached under my desk, I found a sack of gobbed candy corn, some pocket change, and seven dilapidated dollar bills he'd put in a brown lunch sack with a note to say,

Dere Ellen

I diding lik the candy but I hope you will. Dont eat it all at one time. If you dislik it you can go to the stor for sum you do lik and thow this korn in the trach.

I cooding go to the stor becaws I am in trobel for mizbeehaven on the way home from your mamas funrel yes terday.

I wisseld wen you need to stay quiat after some body is ded. I pollogize. My daddy sed it was dizrespetfull of me and punnsht me and went to the stor by hisself widdout me but he came bak unmad and sed I culd help him shav tonite. He tole me your mama was a nise womn. Yuse the chang to git som nise foods.

This is the longess ledder in the werld for me. I muss stop.

Your frend,

Stuart.

Seven

ON THE WAY TO THE FAIR, I WAS IN THE FRONT
seat with Laura, reading her a society snippet from
the morning paper about how Ava Gardner, who was
born a few roads over, had arrived for a quiet family
visit, greeted by neatly bib-and-tuckered young kin, who
more or less lost their minds, thrilled with the many sou-
venirs of Spain she'd brought them. When I asked
whether she knew what sans Frank Sinatra or bull fighter
meant, she said, Without them, but what's that scratching in the backseat? Look around and see if Stuart or
Starletta developed hives in their sleep.

The sound came from Stuart's stomach, which from the way he was turned, had some extraordinary lumps I hadn't seen before that had to be causing the noise when his clothes scraped against them. I said, I'd pull his sweater and undershirt up if I didn't still have an eyeful.

It isn't worth it, she said, nothing is.

The nostalgia that kept us from inspecting him came from the summer before when his mother saw my bicycle parked next door and ran inside to pull me out of selling magazines to their profitable neighbor who owned vending machines for a living. She needed me to help her pull Stuart out from where he'd run from her and gotten stuck under his bed in the nude. While she'd been out, her can of instant suntan had accidentally gotten away from him on a white bedspread, after he'd shaved his body so the color would soak in and chopped himself up pretty well in the bathroom. Because he hadn't bled to death yet and he thought his mother was still in town with his little brother Henry, he took his first shave and did some other grooming as well.

We threw him her red robe and pulled him out by the feet, and he came out as such a blow to the system that you could call home the dank underbelly of a city dripping continually and never see anything like it. She yanked the robe closed on him and tied it harder than Luther's mother ties the bobcat to the tree before a vacation. With him afraid to talk, we had no way of knowing why there were frozen green peas packed in his ears until we realized he'd reamed and gouged around with his father's ear trimmer and figured he was trying to freeze the end of his blood vessels. Stuart's mother had me ride Henry to the store in my bicycle basket and let him eat candy, watching to be sure he didn't expose what was happening at home, to give her time to bleach him.

I couldn't account for today's scratching or the odd shape on Stuart's belly, but I knew when I found out, the news was going to be out where Stuart usually reached, and complicated. All week, he'd been promising to bring a hundred dollars to be a gentleman with. When he'd fallen asleep wedged around Starletta, I read Laura the list he'd given me when just after dawn his mother had slowed down her car and rolled him, staggering, into our front yard. I doubted he'd accumulated the money, and he absolutely hadn't found more spelling skills, but he'd been sure to plan.

What I Tend to Do With Ellen and Show Her To

Slingin rides I love to wach but you couldnt pay me
to ride—Wach with Ellen
Childrun tendin there flocks of sheeps and other
barnyeard animals—Wach with Ellen
Presdents faces painted on eggs, Stachu of Liburty
painted on eggs—Show Ellen
Peecocks, monkees, Sonny and Cher, exhotic beests of
the jungul and all made out of everyday kitchen
foods—Show Ellen
Swurl art wher you squrt paint out of catchup squrt
bottles and they spin it into art—Ellen loves art
so leed her to it
Outsize turkey legs and candeed apples—Feed Ellen
Mrs. Tom Thum, the Smallest Woman Alive—Show
Ellen
Doan walk off a way from the grupe, get More Avien
cooky, thank Lora for carrion you, don get fool
into given the shot gun game man all yure
money, don show off for Ellen to see thu you
and run, get to the bafroom befor it gets bad—
Mama sede

After we'd waited in the traffic line and found a parking place, Laura got out, saying she had one nerve that hadn't been danced on and needed to pull herself together with a bench and a Coca-Cola in a bottle before we were swept away too far inside Gate Five, where we had to give the bag of donated canned goods for free entry. After she dampened a place on her hem and wiped grit crystals from Starletta's eyes, Stuart said his eyeballs felt like they were being cut into as well and stood behind Starletta in line, describing how thick his eye matter could be, particularly after he'd slept in daylight.

Laura fluffed her skirt back down and said, Stuart, you don't have a clear idea of how well you'd have to know a person before they'd love to hear you tell that, do you?

He said, Huh, I was just saying is all.

He pulled out his shirttail and then crammed it back in, saying, Nothing, nothing, huh, let's get rolling.

Rolling toward the gate, with him a little ahead of us and sloped completely over, weighted down by the three sacks of cans he'd insisted on carrying, he banked off cars now and then, more off his axis than normal. Starletta doesn't know how heavy she is, and each holding her by a hand, Laura and I heard our shoulders pop when she'd jump and lunge forward. We didn't so much roll as we jerked to the gate. Stuart still looked too lumpy around the middle, but he'd begun walking more and more upright, like the ape to human evolution picture, and while Laura watched him turn in the cans for us, she said, He has some very strange conduct. Is his mother going to allow them to issue him a driver's license?

I couldn't tell her everybody dreaded it because he was there with the tickets, saying, I need to find a bathroom to have any money.

Laura said, Tell me why that is, son. I'm interested.

He told her, It got to where I kept saying I needed to bring a hundred dollars and pave the way for everybody and my mother kept saying I didn't. But you know the man that owns the vending machines that has the house next to me? I took all my and Henry's change and what was in some jars and coats and different places to get him to turn it into dollars, but all he had was quarters, so I said that was fine, and then I remembered what a man on a show did with some duct tape and dynamite one time, so I got home and took care of it so I didn't have to wake up with it to do this morning.

So, she said, you need to go to the restroom and, well, unbind a hundred dollars in quarters from yourself that you slept in.

Yes mam, he said, and even though it's only sixty, I'm still afraid it could hurt. Do you have any lotion with you? Ellen can tell you it's not a story to say I've got sensitive skin.

It always hurts less when you pull tape off yourself, I told him. Just go do it quick and have it be over with. Starletta's about to start spinning, and the next stop can't be the Red Cross tent.

He was gone long enough for us to visualize him sitting in a stall with duct tape stuck to his hands and his pink skin flaming, so Laura stopped a man at the door and asked him, Do you mind handing this tube of lotion to the little big-boned boy in there for me? His name's Stuart, if you don't see him, call him.

Stuart finally came out, glad for the lotion though now with his shirt sticking to him, saying, Okay, ladies, I'm ready to motorvate.

We changed four sandwich bags of quarters into bills and bought all the ride and show tickets we needed for the day. We stopped at the Village of Yesteryear first to find the Moravian booth and have the rest of the day without the pressure of remembering his mother's cookies, which come canned, so there's no breakage in a satchel. The booth was along a rim of other booths and small areas where they displayed folk customs and crafts, so Stuart and I kept Starletta with us while Laura looked at quilts.

People visit the Moravian ladies' booth in droves for the thin ginger cookies they bake on the premises, and although they're high, if you decide it's too much to ask, you'll wait a year because when the fair closes, they pack up the ovens and journey back to their own world in the western part of the state. They can be compared to the Amish in many of the ways they carry on their affairs, but they contrast on accepting the modern car and the electricity that enables them to have the kind of massive baking operation they were running that morning.

Starletta had on a yellow plaid waisted dress with a green belt, white fold-down ankle socks and blue tennis shoes, and you could tell she'd struggled against her mother believing that colored girls need to go out matching more than most and had won on the dingy striped sweater she took off and tied around her shoulders when she got overheated sucking cookie crumbs up out of what appeared to her as a convenient trough on the side of the Moravian table. I told myself the Moravian lady glaring like I'd wound Starletta up and turned her loose would end once Stuart made his purchase, but Stuart's beading sweating and mumbling told everyone in the booth to come get a load of this boy. Stalled, frustrated, he asked me, Ellen, how many pounds is it to the can? Mama said three pounds, but the label says it's so many ounces to the can.

If he can keep to a rhythm he knows well, he's fine, but off it, he suffers, and worse in public, when he must feel so much farther away from his father, who he craves to be in charge of him on the few days a month he's not away tracking down rubber. The last time his father was home, he told me Stuart had outlined a future with me, saying to please be careful of Stuart's tenderhearted emotions until they passed and also stay safe, avoiding offers to go out in his raft. In fact, he told me I should turn down any invitations that involved his son and fire, outside the rubber pile, experiments with kites in thunderstorms, fishing off the bridge or in their canoe, and overall, any open body of water.

A Moravian lady refilled the crumb tray to see what Starletta would do, and about the time she was down into it hard with both hands to scoop, I said, Stuart, we need to get out of here. Get three cans and let's go.

He took out his billfold, and had me turn from the table while he whispered in my ear, Is what she's cramming in free? I bet she's tooken five pounds. I'll get the three for home and one for each of us, so that's, huh, seven. It sounds like too much to carry though, but, huh, I'll take your satchel.

That's very thoughtful, I told him, but you ought to let that be it and not worry about paying for other things during the day. We didn't come expecting it, so offer to repay the lady on Starletta while she's making out the ticket, and she'll say never mind it, so that'll be all.

Stuart took it in and told the lady, I'd like to go ahead and, huh, give you what you take for seven cans, if you'll let me, and see if I mighten ought to get straight with you on the samples.

He sounded like an old country man, ordering at a sit-down restaurant, because it was how he knew to be right then, and you could tell the lady knew it. She didn't have to stop Starletta by taking the tray up and rush cleaning, and she didn't need to refuse to tell him the price and make him stand there with his billfold open while she finished sizing us up as being the overscrubbed little colored girl with the hundred plaits and plastic bows in her hair, shoving in pricey crumbs she couldn't have at home because welfare didn't pay for sugared snacks anymore. She saw the sweaty, pumpkin-headed boy in husky corduroy pants and a hot-looking boiled-wool jacket with both shoes overflowing with bandaging he'd thought ahead to prevent blisters with. To her mind, neither he nor the colored girl had been anywhere, unlike the girl between them, who'd been to some places and learned how not to look like a tourist, conceited enough to have chosen clothes to make her look slightly above the grime and grist, and also quick-eyed the way tight situations teach you to be. That surprised her, I could tell by the way she looked at me and kept Stuart needing. I was standing there just as dumbstruck as he was.

I couldn't move for the wall I hadn't expected to find that day, at least not so early and at a religion's booth. If Laura didn't swoop in soon, I saw myself leaving some figure of money on the table with the kind of note you imagine writing to people who absorb the day-to-day bravery you need to get around with, saying, You're in a costume, taking money from strangers at the fair. What harm would it do to be decent? You have a bad grease stain on your left chest. Hide and watch it come out in the wash.

Before I saw Laura with her hands on Stuart's shoulders, I heard her say, There's so much clang and clatter in here, so let's make this quick. Let's say what's owed and bag it, but I need one extra can, please.

She paid and then opened the can and poured the

cookies out onto the sampling tray, saying, We're even now. You think?

We didn't talk on the way out, and before we got back in with the stream of people, Stuart had us stop so he could take Starletta's pumpkin pin off her collar and switch it to her skirt so she could handle it without her chin to her chest, running into people. Then standing up, he told Laura, The lady had mean coming to her, huh, you burned her.

She said, I didn't tell her to have a nice day is all, as you say. It sounds rude to omit what people know to be a lie, but you didn't need to carry her out in the satchel.

Starletta was drawn toward where a migrant-looking boy was calling out for fresh swirl artists at his booth, so we all kept the color bottles directed while she squirted with her eyes closed and then became so fixated watching them swirl that although her eyes were opened, the boy said, The little girl, she sleep on her feet.

Stuart said a Methodist hot dog would wake all our moods up, and when Laura and I didn't know what they were, he tapped his back pocket and said, I swear before God, I'd love to introduce you to one.

They were unusually juicy, and while Laura went across to buy a football team hand towel to tie around

Starletta, Stuart said, You know the taxidermy booth? The reason I know so much about out here is Luther and Harvey and me spent the night in it last year and it was next to the Methodists then so when they closed up, they allowed us to take ten, fifteen for a constellation prize after Luther worked like he did on the raccoon and had the letdown when they wouldn't let him run something that wild and not know if it had been rabid or not.

What was he supposed to stuff, I said, a dog? His father had wolves riding around in their old car, drying with the top down.

He was still explaining something about a mysterious film the judges had seen on the animals' eyes when we'd all left to walk down the main way, eating, with Starletta switching her narrow tail and looking fast and terrific, chewing without the bib Laura couldn't put on her, and looking up to follow the voice she knew belonged to the weatherman. The closer we got to the television tent, the more you heard women's voices, saying he's good-looking but not striking, he's secretly married, he's too tan and his suits fit too much like rubber, his face looks rubber, embalmed, reading aloud off the information tables about how he boasts a master's degree in science and loves to cook and fly radio control airplanes.

We stood for Starletta to meet him with some women who seemed to be dreaming of how they'd insert him onto their sofas and discard the men who were leaning against the tent poles to wait. When I edged Starletta to the side of the line for a better view of him signing autographs, she cut out and found an alley between two tents to stand and look petrified in.

I told Laura you couldn't predict it, but her mother said this happened when Starletta recognized a salesman from his used car lot commercials and squatted to hide in fear beside a car. She'd thought the weatherman would be sized to fit the television set. She came out when we told her we'd go to the pick-up ducks booth next, the most luring thing she'd go along with, and then we stayed there through twenty dollars and noon. In the midst of corrupted nastiness of unfair games and people in public with threatening sayings on their shirts, we fell under a spell of mesmerization, watching the ducks streaming by, and when I felt Starletta's wet hand on mine, I fell deeper in to wonder if she understood what her body was making mine remember, my mother's hand on mine, under warm, soapy water, searching around for the chain on the stopper after we'd washed combs and brushes on Saturday mornings. When we were ready to go and waiting for Starletta to fit her fingers out with prize rings, Laura asked what was the matter, and Stuart said, Huh, I think you look patriotic.

I said I'd be fine, but I'd prefer taking the long walk to the slow rides and miss the sights of the slinging ones. It's another kind of ambition that makes you consent to be strapped down on the edge of a rickety circle and slung around to yell like you're glad to be there. I don't scream except in shock or squeal over anything pleasing. I enjoy the sharp pleats on the high school cheerleaders' uniforms, and I like it that our pack of rural girls can flip around and keep the pace in time, but no matter how hard they shout to shout back and go through their set of large arm motions with them, I have to stand there, remembering to smile and clap at the end, hoping it looks like the planet that assigned me to observe this pep rally has rules against me getting whipped up in the action. If startling jolts and frenzy could be eliminated, I could almost be comfortable, the way people with reptile phobias must feel more relaxed living in Ireland. I wasn't as afraid of shooting straight down from a wild ride as I was of my seat cracking off the spoke and shooting me out over the fair. If you've had it happen before with things jerking and shaking off the rails and speeding up before you were thrown outward, you don't acquire a deliberate ticket on centrifugal force.

Starletta rode around on several small, quiet circles, and then Stuart narrated us around the exotic carved and molded food creations in the food building, not saying what he knew, but what he wished he knew about how the things were formed, and when he fixed on a lard replica of Iwo Jima, which had won, he said, Huh, now that's a hobby. You ready to go see Mrs. Thumb?

Laura said she wasn't, so she took Starletta to meet us there later, going off one way while we went the other, irritating long way toward the oddity and striptease rows. Starletta's mother had told me she heard they keep them so far to the edge because the Bureau of Agriculture leader in charge of organizing it had a loud civic wife who drew the fair plan on a napkin.

Nothing's worth this, I told him. She'd better not be on her knees in a long dress.

He stopped walking and blurted, If you think you're better than people like Mrs. Thumb, can you try to hide it harder so I can have a good time?

Stuart, I said, I never know what to do when you decide to let me in on an argument you've been having for us.

He said, But don't tell me you weren't thinking what I said.

Some of it, I told him. I'd be ashamed to tell Starletta's mother we inspected people like slavery.

He said, I knew you'd dislike it in one way, but the other way, I thought you would because you go for unusual things. It's confusing to be walking along, not knowing if you're going to make me like it or despise it. You behave better than me and I'm the one that knows your aunt and cousin are moving somewhere the first of November because Dora's expecting.

When he said the news came from his mother and was beginning to circulate around, I said, You should've let me find out random so I wouldn't attach it to you.

I know, he said, but I swear before God, Ellen Foster, you take a great deal out of people. You want to see her or not?

I asked, Mrs. Thumb or my aunt?

Both, he said, I supposed I imagined.

I said, I can't think to tell whether I have a choice on either, but we're almost in the oddity zone.

When you'd mention what you wanted or didn't want around my father, he'd say to spit in one hand and wish in the other one to see which one got full first, to forgive himself for having nothing to do with how things could turn out for you. Spit would roll through my fingers before anything I wished about my aunt was accomplished. No one was going to hold my Aunt Nadine down while I screamed over my mother's missing things. No one could hold the universe down until it explained why my life had been this particular one and how the rest of it could happen without work taking over and being a secret insanity I'd have to keep hidden to get along in ordinary ways, and particularly in case a man I might love would have me. Males lean toward females with better histories, and although it would be ideal, it would be a rare thing to find one who wouldn't say my history's too freakish for his taste and move on.

Waiting in a long ticket line, I wasn't sure whether I wanted more to leave the misery or injure the people who'd forced me to be inside it more. We didn't mind running to Mrs. Thumb's house with the tickets because the line had drained our time down to a few minutes before the hour, but when we got there blowing, the people coming down her steps said none of the human and animal shows had a set time. You showed up and looked in on her daily life and stayed until she ran you off. When our turn came to group around the short door, she was sitting on her sofa flipping through a True Story magazine with her bare feet propped on one of the stuffed Dalmatians you win throwing darts nearby, fuming.

Stuart whispered, She's got painted toenails. Look, her feet look like the knotted cedar they make lamps out of.

She slammed the magazine down in her lap and said, You talk to your wife like that?

It was sickening to hear the boy's tone when he'd said human and animal shows, but I kept looking because it felt interesting and I had to, despite what Starletta's family from another century had no doubt been put through on slave examining blocks, and what kind of impression I would've made on a human being in the market for another human being.

I touched Stuart's arm and told him never to tell Starletta's mother we were stooped in this door. Stuart was telling Mrs. Thumb, They must take you to the beauty shop every so often, not that you need it though. I was just thinking, huh, everybody's got to get out the house sometimes. It couldn't be healthy, to be shut up. I see you have a fireplace. They keep the chimley working for you?

She glowered at us and twisted around to stand up, so I thanked her for having us, but as we hit the bottom step, we heard her rumbling to the door and shouting,

Nope, nope, nope. You didn't stay long enough to leave and not buy something first.

That's okay, I told her. We're fine.

Pulling some pictures out of a low mailbox by the door, she said, I know you are, growny girl, but you don't want your husband to feel guilty for not buying you a picture of me and President Nixon, autographed, a dollar. I don't think he'd want Mrs. Thumb going hungry, so how about bringing me a couple of Methodist hot dogs?

Stuart stepped up and reached a dollar to her and took the picture, saying, I appreciate it. What would you like on your hot dogs?

I said they must have people who come by with lunch and things of that nature, but she said, Nope, they don't deliver out here.

Stuart asked though not with much zest, What could you call for if they did?

After she said she'd take two with mustard and ketchup, slaw, onions, pickle relish, and chili, it shouldn't have felt like news but it did when she listed what she wanted to go with them, French fries, a large grape soda, two candy apples, and an elephant ear. She didn't offer money, which Stuart chalked up to her not knowing the correct amount, but waiting for her order at the variety foods booth, I looked at the picture and told him, I think we just bought Mrs. Thumb a free lunch.

For mercy, Laura's knack of knowing what to do about hard adults was working well enough to attract her and Starletta to be waiting on the bench in front of Mrs. Thumb's house when we got back overloaded. Looking like it wasn't anything she'd ever believe, she said, When I asked the lady if she'd seen you, she said two bright young people had offered to go pick up her lunch, and I could sit over here and wait, and look at a photograph of her and Richard Nixon. I'll take the food in to her. How much does she owe you?

Thanks, I said, this was about all the Hansel and Gretel ordeal I could take.

We stood on the porch with Starletta while Laura hunched around inside the house, making sure the foods were in Mrs. Thumb's reach, and when she noticed a picture of Mrs. Thumb and Richard Burton on the wall, she said, Nixon, not my type, Burton, definitely, but how did you become such a celebrity?

Not aware we were outside the door or not caring, she said, chewing, Not one. Have a nephew, does put-together pictures for a living.

Laura smiled and said, Well, it's good to have something to make up for everything, and I'm sure lunch would go a long way if I wasn't going to need five dollars for it. Do you keep your money in a particular place? Can we locate that now and get this taken care of?

Laura came out and handed me five dirty dollars, and after she'd asked Stuart to stop repeating, We got tooken, she said, We'll go around some more, but this day will come to a close only after Starletta's looked at some sheep, or goats, and a couple of other very plain, nonverbal things.

After Stuart said he'd love to go now, I said, You don't know how fine that is by me, and I know I need to be extremely nonverbal right now, but I have to tell you what Stuart told me about my aunt moving with my cousin somewhere on account of she's pregnant. What am I supposed to do about it?

Nothing, she said, but find Starletta something slow to pet.

I said, But we need to stop a minute. I don't know if this news can get chopped off like the Moravian lady.

Looking at her neck now because she'd turned her face to the sun and interrupted me to tell Starletta she should try it, which made Stuart look up and leave me with three disinterested throats. I said, Laura, you need to look and let me say I meant what I heard about my aunt and cousin is close to being a bulletin from this other world I had to be in for a while, and I've learned it's scheduled to go to another part of the universe and take some very important stuff of mine with it.

She said, But what we should do, Ellen, is have the remainder of the day here without borrowing interruptions. I know you're eager to talk about it, and we can in a little while. I'm only suggesting you take advantage of the peace we came to walk around in some to recover from the hoopla.

I said, I'll try, but we can't postpone delving again. We could delay Dora if we had to because it isn't like I can do anything but wonder who the father is, whether she's going to finish her education, how her mother's treating her, things like that, but I can't wait and let them permanently steal the belongings of my mother's they took from me. I can't let that happen.

It won't, she said, but nothing's happening now except us walking to the pastured barn area.

I told her I'd like to look for the demonstration cow I'd seen in the paper when he was a feature in the veterinary barn last year. He wasn't there, but the summary is he had hi-fi-speaker-looking circles in the side of his body that monitored his digestive track, but the last thing we saw that afternoon was what a vet told me was the cow's capable replacement. Without saying where the cow went, he motioned toward a clean floored pen with a sign on the gate that said,

Meet Susan!
1974 Medical Miracle
Bovine Research Leads the Way
Support Our Vietnam Vets!
Vets for Vets!

From what her keeper described to us, the farmer who owned Susan took her to the veterinary school because she had a place that was found to be cancer in what would be our thigh. There appeared to be no way to save her, but then a surgeon said he could try something different if the farmer was willing.

I said, Which he had to be, of course.

Yes, he was willing to do what it took, so Susan got her surgery as volunteer to have the section of her leg with the place on it removed and replaced with a mechanical leg section. She has an improved ability to go around in the pen and small pastures and though she hobbles, you think, anybody would and all the best to her regardless.

Eight

ON THE WAY HOME, THE CHOICE WAS TALK TO Laura about the only two leftover members of my family leaving and taking all my mother's things with them or put myself to sleep with the droning tires, so I slept and didn't wake up until Stuart was staggering out of the car the way he'd staggered in. As level as Laura was, if the news had been news to her, she would've shown it. She'd known and had time for it to go through her system to where if you could look into her like the vets looked into the cow through her hi-fi-speaker-looking-deal, the view would've been of calm, eased, normal flowing.

Starletta's mother needed to know about Dora and Nadine. I doubted she did. As much as she was looped into what took place on our road, people like Stuart's mother didn't phone up colored women with gossip. When Starletta's mother came to pick up Starletta with her car and new driving license, Laura and I looked over both the way you do and then came in to round up Starletta and her fair things from my room. I told them, I need to know something first though and what I'm supposed to be doing about it.

Starletta's mother sat on the tall stool by the kitchen window Laura uses to smoke menthol cigarettes out of, with me thinking, She may want to light one up now. Sitting at the table, Laura said, What Ellen's talking about is this business Stuart told her, understanding his mother's the source of truth, about Ellen's Aunt Nadine moving to Texas with her daughter, who's pregnant.

While I was rolling back through Stuart's words, searching for Texas, Starletta's mother said, I hope Ellen's going to get everything Nadine took of Shine's before they go.

Laura opened her mouth to let out what she knew about it but stopped when I sat down by her to say, Texas? He didn't say a specific state.

Ellen, she said, it doesn't matter what I knew or didn't. I don't care to count angels.

Starletta's mother opened the narrow cabinet and felt around for the Kools she and every other woman on the road knew were there, saying, The trick is the angels are on Ellen's pin.

I cracked a window while Laura lit the cigarette that landed on the table and said, What am I supposed to do for relief?

Nothing, Laura said. I'm managing this.

Managing to get throat cancer, I told her. You can smoke one a week and fall to it, but this time when I hit the road, it'll be the highway to Texas. I suppose I could nursemaid Dora's baby and crank my old Cinderella lifestyle back up, although if they're hauling my mother's things with them, I can pick a lock and sit in a Texas attic and heatstroke out while I handle them.

When Laura said, The truth is not so bad, Ellen, that you need to create a story and worry yourself with it.

Starletta's mother said, Then tell her the story. And tell me, I'm interested.

Okay then, she said, so your cousin was running with some . . .

Criminals is what I heard, Starletta's mother broke in.

Probably to get attention, I said.

And, Laura said, she ends up pregnant, and that's all I heard for a while, from Stuart's mother.

She dotes on untimed expectancies, I said, so this is fairly typical for her. Unless Dora murdered her mother and replaced her with a pod person twin, she's still under her mother's same thumb, so you feel one way and another about her having something of her own.

She could've gotten knocked up in the unconscious, Starletta's mother said. It wouldn't be the first time a girl let herself loose with the panty girdle.

Laura smiled, saying, Tell Ellen what you're going to study when you start with the college courses next summer.

Social work, she said, but if I told them I've been with Ellen Foster all her life, I'm sure they'll want to graduate me right away, especially after I hear Laura say what the story is on your family this time.

Another cigarette flew to Laura, but she only rolled it around and stared at it until she looked at me and said, So, I didn't say anything about your cousin because I didn't want to stir all that around, not after you'd just mailed everything to Harvard, and we were working on, well, you have difficulty taking things.

Starletta's mother wet her cigarette out in the sink and threw it away, saying, She's right on that, Ellen, like the AA crowd, one thing at a time.

When Laura motioned for her to pull out the chair beside me, like she could use a person closely present, I said, I know my father's brother died last year, and everybody else is dropped off the face, and Stuart's mother stays out of her mind, but she wouldn't be trading gossip with a ghost, so that's it for people left to die. The ordeal list is down to I'm adopted or my father's alive and married to a striptease, or maybe Starletta's my sister, and I'm way light, or my aunt broke the news that I'm an octoroon on her way out of town, which means paving my way stops being a fight, and I notify the United Negro College Fund.

Laura said, I know, Ellen, there's a world of possibility, twists, and hard angles, but it's straightforward, or would be, if anything before you came here wasn't so loaded, I mean.

Heavy, Starletta's mother said, and you're still sore-armed from carrying everything damaged.

Yes, Laura said, but you see, I called your aunt when I heard about the move and told her to get your mother's things together while she was packing the house, and I'd come by for them. I believed that would end it. She said she'd get some boxes together, but she needed to bring them to you, and it would take a week or so. I said you didn't need it, and if she didn't want me at her house, she could take them to Martha's store, or Starletta's, or even her lawyer's office, if she was anxious about anything valuable in it. So she and her daughter are coming, soon, and I was trying to find a way to prevent you going through that.

I was thinking this was too much vanishing, and if I didn't see my mother's sister, my arms would always have the feeling of a tight need to grab her and make her apologize to me. When Starletta's mother nodded her head down like a prayer and then lifted her eyes up and sighed, I knew she would say what I needed in my life.

Laura, she said, I understand, but Ellen may need a say, not a showdown, just the chance to say a few words and know they were heard. You and I know she spends a great deal of time in her mind, and she may feel due a chance to open it to an individual that stands for all the other individuals that put so much pain in there.

I was trying to arrange some way for you to avoid it, Laura said. That was going to be my job this week, but if you want to see your family, tell me. Keep in mind though the damage if you picture a tender moment or some weepy apology.

Starletta's mother said, I think what happened blows through Ellen's mind fairly regularly.

It stayed, I said, and you know I wouldn't put my hands to her any way she'd enjoy.

Nadine is a cruel wreck of a white woman, Starletta's mother said, and she deserves to be shaken, but she was Shine's sister. She and her mother went berserk because they couldn't watch Shine dying, slipping down, over so much time and them not able to get her out from inside it to safety. They came out of the funeral home swinging with Ellen in the way, and I'm not saying they shouldn't have stopped and said she's Shine's and taken her, because they should've, but Shine wasn't an ordinary person, Laura. She wasn't like you or me. She fairly glowed, and you watch a light like that go out, and it will absolutely drive you to Satan for help fixing revenge. But strip all that away, and this is still Ellen's family.

When I was little, I believed that tears formed one at a time and rolled over my eye ledge, and closing my eyes had to be enough to make them stay back. Glad not to see, hearing was adequate when Laura said, But she's my family, you see, I was here, keeping the house filled, my mother gone, father gone long before her, right here where they left me. And this girl came to me, you see, I didn't believe it, at Christmas, and I didn't know if she was real, you know, because of the way there's something so large about her, and what you say about the glowing of Shine's nature, well, the girl glowed too. And what she told me was so goddamn horrifying, walking up here from her aunt's house, but she was here, and I have been so honored she stayed. I've pulled myself out of many blue days just by saying I must be all right, there must be something right about me, if a person this rare and good chose me.

Taking her hand, I told her, I did, I will.

And you will, she said, do the most amazing things, and what I do, I mean, my life has been keeping a circle around this house, and I can't tolerate the thought of it being broken by anyone who does not wish you well.

When Starletta's mother's said everyone knew what Laura had done, how she'd done what other people couldn't or wouldn't, she was starting to say how the court wouldn't allow her and her husband to take me, and Laura looked at her, not listening, saying, We had a peg-leg man come and build a library. We've waited for box-top packages to arrive from Battle Creek. We've traveled.

We've written to Liberace. I'm on this road it'd kill many people to live on. They'd drop from boredom, but I never thought my life would ever be this interesting. Doing nothing with the child can keep me fascinated and content, and nobody who has done that for me, glad to do it, not aware, is going to be subjected to treachery, you know, that manipulative evil her aunt thrives on without an ounce of guilt, entirely corrupted. I'd blow up the road that runs by here before I'd let anybody get on it to come here with a mind to finding any redemption or doing Ellen any more damage. There's a circle around this house, and anybody who doesn't wish her well has to cross me to get to her, and these are people, a family, allegedly, and I'm her mother now, and I think there's been a goddamn enough. Okay? Is it plain? Was I heard?

She said she was going to lie down and not wait for answers, and after Starletta's mother sat in my room and played with Starletta on the floor, she got up, saying, You understand you're finally lucky, right?

I said I hadn't known, and she said I did now, and to stay to myself and let Starletta and her run to the meat counter and bring back a cold supper. She said, I'll lay out some meats and cheese before I go home, and I'm telling you, it's going to feel like a funeral house around here for a day or more, whether there's pickup food on the table or not. If they sold flowers, I'd buy those, too. I imagine you know what reverent means. You need to be reverent. You need to stay still as you can, and I don't care if you have to imagine it real like these people believing wonders work in coffee grounds and clouds, or fix it like a story you'd write, but you have got to believe a woman who'd blow up the road and die for you had to be sent by Shine. So rest in here with a book to read and let this be a quiet house.

It wasn't possible for the house to be anything but hushed and lowered in the atmosphere though not like after a death. I knew it too well, the way I'd felt when I'd go into a house to sell magazines and be told I should come back in a few days, and knowing without being told that someone is in the back badly fevered or crying. You could tell when you walked in Stuart's house and found him making his brother a sandwich on a paper plate, being careful to use the trash can, that his mother was being tormented by moods her revolving hormones created and used to take her over with. I'd crack open her door to see if she needed anything, and she wouldn't be phoning around gossip or rambling through her purse for something in the second household she claimed to be running in there. She'd be on her side, staring at the window, not seeing anything out of it, and not quite seeing me when she'd say, Nothing, but thank you, I'm fine.

I didn't open Laura's door the rest of the evening, but I did in the morning, and when I asked if she didn't want to take off more than her shoes, knowing her stockings were twisting around her, and get under the top cover at least, she turned her pillow over for the cool side and told me thank you but she was fine. Starletta's mother hadn't said to clean, but it was Saturday morning, which is what we did, and when I took out the products and rags and waited, Laura not coming out was like the woman in the movie who's waiting for the man at the depot, and when one train after another comes without him on it, she has to decide whether to fill out a missing persons report or throw her hands up and start up another love.

I went through the front of the house, my room, and since not running the vacuum cleaner or doing the back rooms created extra time before American Bandstand, I cleaned the car from the fair and outlined what to say to Dr. Bok about how I'd gotten ahead of myself and probably should stay home for now. I'd meant to have it ready for the mailman, but he came while I was inside the car, with nothing but the box of sample magazines. I bathed and crawled onto the sofa with them, not wanting to read anything that would excite ideas enough to break through a time I'd sworn I'd keep quiet.

Starletta's mother called, saying she was sorry to make the phone ring, and I told her I was as well on account of it went off like a shot. I asked if it was all right to slip a note under Laura's door to remind her about a new comedy show coming on late that night, something we'd emphasized not missing. She said it was fine but leave it at that, and if Laura got up to make supper, help around the edges, but don't treat her like an invalid and take over. She suggested fresh air, so I rode the cookies I'd found in the car down to Stuart's house, but no one was home, so I sat on his bucket and poked at the rubber pile and rode back home, and when I opened the door, I saw what Laura meant when she said we'd made something whole. It would've been whole if every gorgeous thing had been hauled away while I was out, and the air in there would've felt this right weight of solid, because, I knew now, it was made of the air we breathed there.

It would've made the next days easy if I'd believed I'd wanted my mother's things only to touch my hands to what had been inside of rooms she and I were in, when my father was absent, and the air felt like this. I could've told Laura I agreed that my aunt didn't need to come, so don't let her, and if you don't get my mother's belongings, let them go on to Texas, but I wanted them in my hands. And I wanted them in case I had a girl to come open the door of my room to ask if I needed anything, and I'd have the capability to tell her I needed her to sit on the side of the bed while I gave her some small belonging of my mother's. There's life in things. There's life in everything. My mother won't be there to give my girl her heart, and I know she would, so I'll have to. I'll have to do what my mother would've done, say what she would've said, Come here and let me show you something, this is what I have for you because I love you.

I wanted to remember my mother telling me she loved me. She did, you know she did, but I couldn't hear the words. Laura had said everything around it, so had I, though if I'd said it, until now, it would've been a lie. I loved her being there, loved watching her, and I loved that she didn't seem to have a history, how she seemed to have been invented the day I walked into the house. I loved that she was a woman who hid women from laundry and loud boys in their houses, and I loved how she once calmed Starletta's aunt when she came to help us get ready for new kitchen cabinets and brought along her infant who was wailing, hungry, but her mother was too jazzed, she said, by some nasty life events that had taken place right before they got here so she couldn't relax and let down. Laura had her lie down on her bed, and after I'd made hot compresses from the good hand towels and made the woman a glass of chocolate milk, Laura repaired her with the milk and the wet heat.

The young woman said, It won't ever be any better than this. Then she sighed so long and hard, the wind fluttered the baby's hair, and she held her to her chest. Laura paid her for work the two of us did and paid her not to come back and do more. After the girl had been on the payroll a few weeks, she had to move with the man who'd upset her, but she sent Laura a thimble made by Starletta's mother, which is how I remember her, when I hear her sigh when Laura sews.

Laura set out leftovers and took a plate to her room, telling me she'd feel better in a while and come out for the show, and if I wanted to make a pallet on the sofa, since we'd be up late, that was fine. She'd seen the note and was glad for the reminder. I gave her a handful of things I'd torn out of the magazines, telling her one of them was about women writing love letters to Charles Manson. She smiled and said their mothers must be proud, and then she set her plate on the table and told me, You know another thing about this house? There hasn't been a man here, not to stay, since my father left it, and that has to account for how bad it feels when there's a struggle, there's been nothing to accustom the place to fear.

I said, I don't want you to think I'm afraid you'd let me get hurt.

She said, And you know that.

When I said, Absolutely, she said, Okay then, move over. Phyllis Diller's on a special this evening. Did you know?

I hadn't known it, but when we located the program we began laughing and decided to be irresponsible and let the room go, and when the late comedy show came on, she said she couldn't listen to me anymore until she'd gotten down the thesaurus and found synonyms for amazing. We talked about a million people with the popularity boxes voting the show off and said we'd burn for being conceited and then came down a peg when we didn't know who Buck Henry was despite how he no doubt couldn't walk roads elsewhere without being mobbed. But, I told her, I know enough. I know why you want to close the door to what happened. We've had October in this house.

Nine

O N SUNDAY, WE DROVE TO THE VERGE OF THE mountain part of the state, where potters hold open houses and invite people in to observe them at the wheel and ask questions. We walked around, bought some of their wares, and had supper at a Shoney's. Tired, we got home after dark to find Stuart's bicycle leaned against the front steps and him sitting there waiting, squinting at us in the dim porch light, with a paper sack in his hands. Laura said to pray for a second wind to blow through, and then we took our new vases out of the car, pulled his bicycle out of the damp, and invited him in.

Watching him slope to my room, Laura said, Just pay

some attention to him, and make sure there's nothing alive in the sack.

He'd been crying. He told me nothing was the matter, he only needed to talk to me privately before he died. He closed my door and laid his coat across the foot of my bed, and then he flopped back on it and looked at the ceiling, asking, Would you mind? Huh, I swear before God, I wish you wouldn't. If you do, you'll need to allow me to stay here until I get up.

In case he rolled over, I sat against my pillows and asked if the reason he'd been crying had to do with the sack, which was moving up and down on his stomach. The sack, he said, came after Mama hit me like a man. She said it was coming and dared me to run. I should of left before she did it, but later on, I told her I had to go see a man about a dog, and then I rode on up here. You didn't say you'd be gone.

So you waited how long? I asked him.

I hadn't needed to ask about the dog because people say it when they don't want you to know where they're going, usually to get a present for you. He'd slept off and on outside the house, he wasn't sure how long without a clock, but he said he'd definitely been out there from can see to can't see.

When I asked how things turned out with the dog, he said, I got it, but I need to tell you first I hauled heaving outside your house. The rain they said was coming tomorrow, should take care of it so you don't have to stand elsewhere and wait on the bus, but, huh, I think I broke some ribs, and my lips dried. Does it look like I'm going to get a blood blister?

I said, You could use some Vaseline, but please fold your lip back up before I have to remember Luther's attractive cousin.

He couldn't listen for feeling over his skin and mashing around to make sure, he said, his mother hadn't injured him beyond whiplash when his head spun around.

I said, Stuart, your mother, I know, has a hard time when she gets to the end of her rope, like yesterday, when she rolled you out of the car. Do you need Laura to try and find your father at one of those places he stays at on the highway?

No, he said, she wasn't trying to kill me yesterday. She was running late to be early in line for a store closing holding a special. She dislikes for you to move slow. One reason she likes you is you go in high gear.

Laura had once called him a nitwit with a heart of gold who would wander the earth unless someone was there to corral him, so when it appeared he'd come to the end of his explanation and locked a gaze on the ceiling with tears shivering over his eyes, I said, Climb up around here by me, Stuart, and let's end the suspense on the sack. I think I need to be complimented for not snatching it.

Yes, he said, you're a patient girl. Knocking against the headboard and shoving a pillow roll behind his neck, he said, The pain may be from squeezing the handlebars with my mother on my mind.

Tell it, I said, I've had the same sensations going on lately about my aunt.

Bingo, he said, on what's in the sack, but before I let you have it, I need to say I wish I'd allowed you to behave your way at the fair. I'm sorry about that now on account of the trouble it caused from what happened when Laura phoned up my mother this morning, early, so it wouldn't eat at her with the two of you out trying to have fun.

When he stalled again and I told him to start with the first memory and work his way through, he said, Huh, okay, so I was in the hall, and my mother, she picked up the phone. I wasn't going to listen until I could tell it was Laura and heard Mama say, It's not a problem for me to tell you what I know. Nadine tells me things like I want to hear them, and if I'd thought it was my business, I would've gotten in touch with you immediately. Nadine knows how I feel about her treating a child like a cur dog, but she feels bound and compelled to talk to me like I've ignored it.

What, I said, was the topic, you know, the theme?

He said, One was Mama telling Laura she would've taken you in to raise if she'd felt straighter after she had Henry and believed she could manage the two she already had, which was a shock to me, and a letdown, knowing you could've been a sister. The other main thing said was your aunt has been running things for your grandmother since she died, and she isn't leaving because of Dora. Dora's the excuse for her mother to be gone when people find out she's been collecting rent from the family that rents your old house that everybody knows you need for school and how you despise taking from Laura. People know that. When they comment on you working like a grown woman, I tell them you go and do on your own and plan to.

I thought the bank owned the house. I thought the man at the bank took over everything that belonged to my grandmother, and she'd left my aunt a chunk to raise

Dora on. She's been in private school. I passed by the shoe store last year and saw her in there trying on leather boots. Is there anything else? Did it sound like it'd be enough to get from now through college and medical school on? Do you mean to say I own the house?

Yes, he said, and I don't know how much she's tooken from you. The last thing I heard was a whoosh from Mama swinging back, but I think she was upset more because she likes to believe Laura thinks highly of her, like they have the same standing, and me telling you got her caught carrying a story. She'd already phoned up several individuals on it though she told Laura she might've mentioned it to one.

I said, I hope it helps to see the reason she hurt you. It's smart of you to know.

Handing me the sack, he said, Smart was taking the Phillips head when I took the other one and left.

Inside the sack was a doorknob I recognized. We had a glass one like this. Did you take it off my old house for me?

Yes, he said, smiling, and I know you're going to ask me why. I planned on saying, huh, to make you ask me questions.

Okay, I said, so if that didn't satisfy me, what did you plan to say next?

He reached over and turned the doorknob a touch and said, It was on the outside, and you've wanted something from there for a long time is the main reason. Then hearing how everything's stirred up again with your aunt, I said to myself, Ellen needs me to give her the doorknob so she can shut all the rooms and close her old house. Don't take it the wrong way, but you live in it so much of the time is what I see. The doorknob is for you to use in your mind, so don't take it over there and try to install it back on because, huh, you have no idea how disappointed your mother would be if she knew how the family kept her house looking inside. They're very common people, Ellen, and your mother was so tall and clean. Keep looking up when you ride by. I'll let everybody know to keep helping you.

I'd made myself not look at the house by making sure someone was always riding beside me if I had to be that far across the river. Martha or Luther, for instance, always told me to quickly notice an odd cloud in the sky, and Stuart liked to say he saw rockets launched from Cape Canaveral. When I asked if the house was completely

decrepit, he said, About, and I couldn't bring a dead pot-
ter plant or string and strowed trash from the yard. Remember when your mother ran out of air blowing up the
pool for us to play in?

No, I said, it's one of the things that slipped through
and now I'm not able.

Don't worry about it, he told me. I've got it for you.
You see, where I remember Miss Shine doubling over,
falling, and you down there with her, giving her breath,
and me running across the road for Starletta's father to
come is where these shiftless individuals have a smoking
pile of trash, not something you'd make a living off of,
Ellen, but like, when they weren't home, I figured they'd
gone to get more garbage to throw on it. No family of
four can create that much trash.

I didn't know how I understood what to do when my
mother fell. Maybe she fainted so often that I'd looked up
directions. I didn't know, and no scenes came back, but
when I was beginning to feel too sunken in from too
much lost, he said, But Ellen, let me tell you what the
good thing was. Let me tell you how it was the same
weather in the yard from where the wind used to pick up
the pecan leaves and cyclone them. The only thing missing when I saw the leaves twirl a circle was you and me

watching Starletta squatted down, reaching out to pat it and her having the blues when it stopped, not meaning to say it was a ghost there on account of I remember the ground there had a habit of cyclones coming on. But remember another thing?

I probably don't, I said, and thank you for these, but they're sufficient. You can get supersaturated. I don't know if your class got to that, I mean I can't use anymore until these absorb.

I ran a experiment on it, he said, with Luther and a glass of water and some sand from the park in town.

When I asked how things had turned out, as he got up and lay the doorknob on my dresser and came back for us to watch it like a display on view, he said, Polished dirt wasn't worth a damn, and since it was a take-home test where the answer was the fastest rate, we dug loam and used it. We'd used town sand to keep from turning in mud, but it wasn't the answer, just a waste of gas, tires, and oil to go get it.

You learn, I said. Then he let me turn on the side with my back to him, and he let us be quiet until he began going through his coat pockets and suggested I sit up and look at the foot of my bed if I wanted the surprise of my life.

Before I did it, I asked if he realized it was Sunday

night and he usually had pajamas on by now, and he said he did, but he was wearing something better. He had his paisley necktie on. He pulled a leg up under him and leaned toward me and said, I meant the doorknob, so don't believe I didn't, and now I need you to trust me on a instadecision I made when Mama took and hit me.

I expected him to say he wanted to start technical school at Harvard, and Henry was dragging his suitcase up the road right now for him to stay with Laura and me in the meantime, but he said, I may not have a ring for your finger. Like said, it was a instadecision, so it wasn't time to go speak to Sears about the extent of me credick.

Did she slap you, I said, in the face or the head? Sears, extend you credit? Do you hear yourself?

I do, he said, and, huh, that's exactly what you're going to be saying to me next Saturday.

On Candid Camera, I told him. Are you going to tell me now or later I'm expecting.

Cart before the horse, he said. I just wanted to tell you I apologize your finger has to stay empty for a while, but allow it to make you feel better to know the man has a very clean truck.

When I asked what truck, he said, The truck the man drives tires in. He has told me I could ride and bring a friend anytime, anyplace, anywhere, so when he comes tomorrow, I'll make arrangements and be sure he knows not to pile anything in the seat next Saturday or ask his own wife to travel with him. It's our day, and, huh, I swear before God, I'm not likely to share it.

Stuart, I said, hold on. We don't have a day.

That's why, he said, I think Saturday's good. We'd spend the night at the South of the Border with the Valentime bed and one that pulls out the wall, which I'd appreciate having because I wonder what it'd be like to sleep on one. Then he'd carry us back here on Sunday. Harvey and Luther said they'd give us a list of what fireworks they wanted.

You told them about this?

He said, I rode by their houses a minute before I knew you weren't home, but don't take it the wrong way. I just said I was going across the state lines with you. I didn't say why, and they said they'd appreciate us bringing them back firecrackers is all. You know you can't beat Pedro's variety, and Ellen, you don't need to worry about me being one of these that run out and play cards and set off explosives with their friends and leave you alone of an evening.

When I said that wasn't what I'd been thinking at all,

he said, I know, I was off on a tange. What I was saying was I'll tell the man to make sure everything's in order and see if he can get the South of the Border church and the motel and lay it to his charge-a-plate if I can't get my mother to sign for me to draw out of the bank this week. She'll sign for a married son though, and I've got fair money to last until then, so, huh, I'd say we're in the right shape, particular since you didn't know how high my bank figure is since a certain grandfather died.

Mother of God, Stuart, I said, did you just wink?

And you'll be getting used to it soon, he said, lesser nerves, lesser mistakes, more of me being the one in the lead.

He more or less fell forward and got me around the waist, so there wasn't a choice but to be there to hear, Oh God, I'm dying to cross the state line with you.

He wouldn't let go when we heard his mother slamming through the door. A man, he said, would tell her he's a man. He'd care for his woman and fix tricky situations.

Stuart, I said, your mother is going to box you. Laura's going to be confused. I appreciate the doorknob, but we'll talk about the other at school.

Sitting up and pulling his arm away, he interrupted

me, saying, Which I forgot to say I want you to keep attending.

Trying to erase the picture of Jerry Lee Lewis and his child bride from my mind, I said, I don't think it's legal anywhere, and you know you don't want me to be an outlaw.

I know, he said, and you know the family that eats off records? The mother changed four birth certifs so they'd take her children in school sooner. One of them sits next to me and looks, huh, seven. How hard could it be? Do you have your certif or did it get tooken from your old house? I could get started this evening.

He didn't care that Laura could be heard calming his mother down in the kitchen. She's not the woman I want running me, he said. And you don't know how I'd take and look after you. You know the colored man who works for Daddy and lives in the little blue house with the roof you said looked like they painted it with chocolate milk? Well, he moved out, so we could move in.

So, I said, I just stay home from college?

He said, They've got one here, and it'd be fine for you to go and be in the house of an evening for me to ask how soon supper is and what you learned and so forth. I mean, huh, it's modern. I mean, I don't picture you at the ironing board, but it's not my fault what I see. That's just the way it is, Ellen. But it's fine on the county college. I wouldn't bother you out of school any more than you'd stop me from opening service bonanza locations up and down the innerstate highway. It won't be the women's lib moving either though. You deserve to live like the lady with the government husband they had on trial that summer when you said you admired how she stayed fixed and said her legs stayed crossed to where she'd hit the floor twisted if she went to stand up.

I said, We're not John and Maureen Dean.

Which reminds me to tell you, he said, glasses run in my family, so I'll be headed to the optimist probably here directly, and I'll see if he carries some like the man had on. Then I'll come in the door for you to say they become me. It'd make you feel more like you'd gone on and gone to Harvard. And long as I'm on the topic, ask yourself if Harvard was the one who showed up here and got you.

Giving me time to settle that for myself, he stared off to listen and gauge how much time we had before Laura had done the most she could do with his mother. I told him quietly, Stuart, I didn't try out for the Harvard foot-

ball team. This isn't like the time the coach came out here
and slept on the couch at Luther's and bought groceries
and outfits for everybody, luring his brother to play on
his team.

He wasn't listening. He turned to me and said, What
I want, for the largest part, is to have a little blue home
with you, Ellen. I was outside it this afternoon, and all
I could think is how pretty you'd look in the yard with
clean tennis shoes on, sweeping a rake. When you're
through, I want to watch you drink a glass of chocolate
milk, and then I want to fry a steak and watch you eat it.
You used to look odd, but I swear before God, you've
gotten very, very good-looking, at least to me. And now,
it sounds like my mother's going to be in here any
minute, but don't say anything. She doesn't know, but,
huh, I'll tell her.

I said, So she finds you missing and hears all this. I'll
leave the two of you alone.

I wish you wouldn't, he said. It'll come out better
with you here. The closest I came to talking to her about
anything on this order was when she talked to me about
women one time and said I should try for the quiet ones
and leave the ones more like you alone on account of you

have to be tough to keep a smart woman from dating out on you.

Everything else he'd been talking about left my mind, and all I could think was how his mother had gotten this warped impression of me. I almost wanted her to hurry so I could ask how she could believe that enough to say it like a fact. I said, She's known me all my life. She should be thinking the opposite. What have I done to make her think that?

Listen, listen, he said, I know you aren't that way. I mean, I wouldn't have to worry about you dating out on me, would I?

No, I told him, of course not, no. You know I'm not the kind of person who'd date out on their husband.

His mother knocked on the door as she opened it and looked hard at both of us. Laura was looking over her shoulder. I was about to ask what I'd said or done to make her think I'd deliberately hurt her son or anyone else, when Stuart shouted, Come on in! It's no time like now to meet my bride-to-be, Ellen Foster! Come on in, ladies! Congratulate me and my honey.

Ten

STUART CALLED AT MIDNIGHT, CRYING. HE CLAIMED that his mother put on a false front in my room and then took it off on the way home and tried to beat him to death with it. He said she'd backhanded him, put out his hearing, and caused him to bleed from the ears, and when I asked whether she'd kept the car in the road, he said, You've heard her say how strong she is from carrying groceries in the house by herself? Well, she is. She's strong armed in both arms and got fairly good aim.

His mother actually had a reputation for being able to drive with one hand and change a diaper with the other one. She was also often called Job, Laura said after they left, for extremely sensible reasons. That could now include being asked repeatedly on her way out with Stuart whether she felt rooked out of planning a grand wedding, whether she'd carry him by the banker's house to get his inheritance, as tomorrow felt all over like too long to wait, and whether she'd accept the honor of our firstborn being named after her. He said, I feel a female coming on, O Mama!

Laura said, Barring killing him and standing over him lying there in his green sweater and prison shoes to give him the worst blow of all, how do you intend to break through this world he's in with the news?

That I'm not marrying him now or ever? I asked.

She said, More than one thing at a time is a thousand times too much for someone that fragile to bear.

One of his themes, I told her, has always been apologizing for something he tried to believe because of pressure from his mother. With anybody else, it'd be an individual versus society conflict, though she tends to come at you with the force of a large group.

So, you think he's going to take it all back?

Yes, I said, and soon. I'll tell him it's okay, but that'll take a while, and I'm tired, so when the phone rings, I may have to not hear it until I get the next wind.

Then lie here with me and listen to something I've had to wait for the next wind to say as well. You need to know, Ellen, I wasn't trying to hide anything from you about your aunt and the house. It didn't feel right to pass along secondhand information that could be contradicted by fact. I was planning to talk to an attorney and your aunt and then come to you when I had things straight. I hope that can be okay. I was looking after your interests, but I'm afraid it feels like I'm making the way to do it up as I go along.

I trusted her, and I told her, You're the one to see what's happening for me. I see it, and it's fine. But what do I do if I own my old house? What if Stuart had it right?

She said we'd decide when she sorted out the truth. After we talked about the state line, the tire truck and fireworks, the ironing board and the blue house, and I was finally in bed, Stuart called. It wasn't in his mother's nature to go at him that severely, but it was in his recent mental makeup to take the phone with the long cord to bed with him and call me saying he'd been direly injured. Love or lust was new to his personality. Four years ago, if you'd have asked him what he wanted, he would've said a new cat and a rainproof tent, and now it was like he had no choice but to let me in on how the torment was tightening the grip.

Blowing his nose, I pictured in the pillowcase, he said, I wanted you to know I won't be in school tomorrow, too shamed, and mad, too, about how you got tooken by your family. I know your aunt's going to bring your mother's things to you, and I know she's got to get straight with you on the owed rent, but I'd appreciate you not mentioning I took the doorknob off the house though I ought to be apologizing to you. I'll put it back on for you this week.

What you did doesn't qualify for cringing, I told him. I'll see you in the morning.

It felt like only an hour passed before I was on the bus in front of Stuart's house, watching Henry get on holding a biscuit. He sat across the aisle from me, splitting it open on top of his spelling book. I asked where his brother was and he said, Fighting with Mama over you in the kitchen. He said his eyes swoll too bad for school. She said, huh, he'd be swoll shut next time he goes up yonder to Ellen Foster's house to be the fool and be crazy.

Henry, I said, what are they saying about me exactly?

I had to wait for him to distribute a packet of grape jelly he'd taken from a massive glass jar of restaurant condiments his father empties his pockets into after a trip

the way people do with their change. Chewing, he said,
She said leave you loam. Said you got it made. Stuart said
you don't. She said he knows half it and to shut up and
put a bag of froze peas on his eyes. Tole him he knows
where they are afore she chunked the bag at him, huh.

By the time we unloaded at the main doors, I'd poked
Henry from every direction, hoping I'd hit something
concrete he'd stored up about what Stuart knowing half
of things meant, but I learned nothing outside of what
height of desperation it takes to ignore your friends
rubbernecking you block a sticky-faced third grader
from his classroom to urge him to say why, from his
point of view, would his mother be saying I had it made.

Martha was at her locker and overheard me asking
him whether his mother might've said I had it made
because I might go to Harvard, trying to see what rang
bells. She said, Ellen, he came in the store Saturday and
shoplifted the cake mix he lives on again. He's Henry.
Turn him loose.

I told him to go on and then I helped Martha stand
there and stare in her locker like you do with the refrigerator door open. The problem was the stacked and
crammed boxes of women's monthly supplies in every
variety from teen styles to things Luther saw and said his

uncle used on horses in heat that she kept on hand for
Mrs. Delacroix and lunchroom ladies Nature hadn't left
yet. When I asked if she needed to use some room in
mine, she said, I don't know. I can't think.

I said, Then did you hear anything in the store about
me having it made this weekend?

No, she said, nothing. All that happened this weekend was Daddy ran across a deal on a car he said I could
have if I helped pay for it. Unless you have it made to
where you want to buy five hundred dollars worth of
Kotex, I don't want to hear about it.

So you didn't hear either, I asked her, about me own-
ing my old house and it not belonging to the bank, nothing about my aunt taking the money off from it?

She said, No, but that's good news. You can evict the
trash that lives in it if for no other reason than they
haven't paid their bill in a year and have the gall to send
a toddler in there to charge groceries. I hope they've been
paying rent. How are you going to get it out of your aunt?

I explained how Laura was going to call a lawyer
that morning and see where things stood, but I said, I
wouldn't be surprised if I was owed somewhere in the
thousands, which is why my aunt's leaving for Texas but
telling people it's because my cousin's pregnant.

the life all around me by Ellen Foster

Walking outside to the low stone wall, she said, That doesn't sound right. She did much worse to you before and stayed here with everybody knowing it.

It hadn't occurred to me, but she was right. I told her Laura would have everything outlined by the time I got home. I felt looser in the neck than usual, knowing something would be made right. Some people already on the wall told Martha and me to look across the road at where they were watching four boys in the high school parking lot while they sat on a tailgate and cleaned shotguns and then sent the skinny one off with two buckets for ice from the lunchroom. They dumped those into a large chest before they unzipped out of their camouflage covers and got their books together to attend classes until it was time to take what they'd shot home and please their mothers with how fresh everything still is. Watching them and listening for our names to call back present, a girl named Mae who rarely talks but to herself, said, I bet that's us next year.

I was stupefied. Then she said, Hey Ellen, my mother was on the same train with you far as Washington. You didn't see her, but I was thinking, if you go on to Harvard, what're you going to do about school?

I said I hated I'd missed her mother and waited for a way to defend myself for dropping out of school, but

151

Luther jumped the wall from behind me and sat, looking down at her. Do you think she belongs here, period? He said, It's not like the truant officer's going to go drag her back from Harvard. How many classes have you seen her in? She's been in the library, already good as gone, and rules don't apply to high-IQ people. She could get the thing the Pope gave the lady in the paper if they took and forced her across the road.

A papal dispensation, I told him, but I don't think it'd get that far, especially with me not being Catholic and not going to church for three years.

Martha said, I think those are for if you get knocked up.

Everybody knew and seemed to tell me at once, Maybe your cousin could get one.

So I asked whether anyone had heard anything about me having it made, and Harvey said, Stuart's mother called mine and said it. After a few others said his mother had phoned up theirs with the same news, I said, All I know is my old house belongs to me, but it doesn't rate the easy life, I don't think.

Luther said, You should fix it up for Marvin to stay in before his house slides off in the river.

I said I didn't know what to do yet, but it was being

taken care of, and I'd ask Stuart directly if the thought of it didn't wear me out. People said, Tell it! Who knows where he is?

At home in the kitchen, I said, too downtrodden to be here.

Harvey said, He came to my house wild yesterday afternoon, and when he said he was going to leave for Luther's and over the pasture to your house, I said I'd better ride with him to make sure they wouldn't have to drag the river with the wide net later that evening. He said he'd bring firecrackers from Pedro's, but you don't know what to believe.

Believe, I said, the only explosions on this road are going to be from Laura going up against my aunt. Stuart had a plan to cross the state line for a strange purpose, but, for mercy, it didn't work out.

Good God, Martha said. Girls who didn't get the Pope excusing the baby, or whatever he does, go for quickie weddings down there. If you're not on the way to Florida or out of explosives, it's why you'd go. I'd imagine Stuart's a bad enough wreck that you'd need to go to Harvard sheerly to escape the hounding on account of he's going to keep coming. Sorry to say it, but the only person I can see you setting up housekeeping with is

Stuart or the one from the book you made us all read, the screwup with the gray hair.

Holden Caulfield, I told her. This is depressing.

But Ellen, Mae said, don't places like Harvard want you to have a sport or a talent or something to make you more well-rounded? Don't take it the wrong way, but anybody can ride a bicycle.

Luther said, Mae, when's the last time you filled out the crossword puzzle or read something outside Guideposts?

I said, I put a letter in with the scores and some themes, saying I hadn't had time to develop a talent. If they call for a sport, you're right, there's the bicycle.

And Ellen, Marvin said, has always had good posture, but Ellen, hey, you think you might allow Daddy and me to rent your house?

I told him I'd have to see what was what, thinking he must be extremely concerned about drowning asleep to want to move into a house that two people had died in and where everybody knew I didn't as much live with my father as hide from him. Despite how the family of four had treated it like a routine rural house to trash, I often wondered if they heard pleading in the walls, great sad sounds you associate with locations in the universe where good and evil and peace and desperation clash.

Mae had been mumbling at the other end of the wall, and when I heard Luther shout out loud, She is too good, and she has to think it, but when's the last time you heard her reminding somebody of it? Do you see her cut out to care what's up with Lottie Moon Society or going out for the softball team? When's the last time you went somewhere to know about how you get to go?

Nowhere yet, she said, but we're going to Colonial Williamsburg for Thanksgiving.

I told Luther not to bother, I was fine, but everybody stopped and tuned in the way they do when somebody says they're going somewhere besides White Lake. Mae said, It's my parents' anniversary, and when my father asked what my mother wanted, she said she wanted to go to Williamsburg and stay where you're not allowed to cook, so he parted the flock early.

I said, You're taking a vacation on chickens?

I wouldn't go to Williamsburg, Marvin said, ducking his head to his shoulder like a horrible memory was coming back. Have you heard how easy it is to fall in a soap vat?

Martha said, When Ellen and me went to Tweetsie Railroad last year, the Indians robbed the train in tennis shoes.

After I added on how there was nothing in the gift store there you wanted, Harvey said, We went to pick my uncle up at the airport once, and you could live on what they carry in the vending machine area if you were out in the woods for a year.

Marvin said, You'd lack a place to plug them in.

But listen, Harvey said, to what happened to this man the time his wife plugged the wringer washing machine in behind his back, jerked his arm through, and mashed him to where his neck went into his head.

What I heard, Luther said, as the teacher leaned out the window and shouted the roll, was the woman mashed the man's peter.

We gathered our belongings to go inside, laughing but squinting, trying to see if the story could be real, how and why the man would've been angled up on the washing machine, except Mae, who had to let us know before we opened the wide main hall doors, My mother's got different tours planned. She wouldn't allow me around a soap vat.

Mine either, I told her. It's a story is all.

Mae, Martha said, can you please turn back into Helen Keller and stop reminding me how if Ellen does leave here, there's nobody to stop a plague of ignorance from taking over?

I didn't have to separate into the library that morning because an assembly was scheduled for the county health nurse to show a personal hygiene film. If I wasn't off to myself, I didn't want to feel both near and far but home, so I said, I need to leave the ill will on the low wall. Being the one they said has it made ought to give me the right to say I'm on the verge of a big sweep of things that's more than likely going to clean away anybody who doesn't wish me well.

Mae said, It sounds selfish. You just want people around that wish you well all the time.

Before I could explain how I hadn't meant I wanted to be with people who told me only what I wanted to hear and how a thoughtless family was back and weighing down on me, Stuart's large arm was over my head, holding the heavy gym door open. Ignoring questions about why he was sore-eyed, I imagined from an ointment he'd applied to hurry the frozen peas, he shouted over the noise inside, What's the topic? Ellen getting to have people that wish her well with her all the time? I think it's a good idea, but I'll be able to say more on it later, when I'm less partway blinded.

When we were seated on the bleachers, when the lights went down and Luther whispered with a kind of

Kaye Gibbons

blowing, damp heat into my hair, Hey, hey, I just thought of the way to train the wild out of the bobcat faster. Treat him like he's already a cat, and he'll get some habits that can sink into him later.

Thinking you could do worse than having Luther wishing you nothing but well, I said, And then, Wa-La, he'll be a pet?

Exactly, he said, behave to him the way you expect him to behave.

I told him it was a revelation, and then we were all told to hush, but knowing we had a few minutes before the health nurse repeated it, Martha spoke over my shoulder, saying, Listen, you've got a head for business. You know how shamed boys are to buy their things? They stalk around the store and wait for one of my brothers to wait on them, and on Saturday nights, town boys come in droves to be incognito, so think and tell me if it makes sense for me to branch out from female supplies to male and get somebody honest like Stuart to sell them next year.

Thinking this wasn't a model conversation for Dr. Bok to know about, unless Martha was about to tell me her idea had its beginnings in Thebes, I said, His brother's sharper, but they've all got another year to get less goofy, so you'd find somebody willing to split a profit

158

hand over fist with you. Isn't it taking money the store could be making?

She said, What I'd make, I wouldn't have to beg for. They still pay me what I find sweeping, but hold the fort and notice it's dark and Starletta's not in your lap.

I had to tell her Starletta's class had been banned because of the sexy subject matter involved with a venereal disease movie. You wouldn't think new state politics would've had the trickle-down effect on us after less than a year of extremely strict people in office, but they'd made certain decisions on church and state and free speech that I didn't mention to Harvard. With of all the things off in my background, saying the library was sent a list of books to remove, which Mrs. Delacroix and I ignored with anxiety, made it sound like the atmosphere was too tinged with danger. Although if you'd seen the books they wanted out, it would've felt like you were tied down and made to hear hostage takers shout warped ideas and lies.

Starletta would've loved to see the husband of the witch in Bewitched playing the captain of a high school basketball team who wrestles with venereal disease. He and his girlfriend are perfectly popular, riding around with the gang crammed into a kind of jalopy automobile, but they don't expose how social he was on a trip to the city before the movie started until he's in the locker room, in despair and pulling his best friend aside to tell him, I've got a problem, down there. They glance down at the front of his uniform shorts, and now they're both looking destroyed in the face but determined to make it through and not risk college or his girl finding out. They decide to involve a hood who's more in the know and says he should get to a doctor on the double.

Then the boy's instantly sitting on an examining table, rolling his sleeve down and thanking the doctor for the shot he just gave him, and then they turn to face you and warn against trading your family, friends, and future for one night of what they both admit sounds like a barrel of fun. A nurse wheels in a blackboard with some statistics listed on it, and after the doctor runs through them, he says if numbers bore you, then the weak-kneed beware and everybody get a load of these close-ups of sores and let them convince you. The boy chimes in then, holding a basketball out of nowhere, to say, summarized, And remember, your teen years are like, say, practice for the biggest game of your life. Sure, make the scene dating, and get to know all types of people, but take it from someone who's been there, abstinence always makes the heart grow fonder.

The music comes on, and he's playing basketball again and smiling at his buddy like he's glad all that's over with and winking at his girl, who's screaming her head off for him, clueless she's soon to be coated in sores down there or gossiped about as the news of how untrue he was to her begins leaking out. You could tell it's all going to end up swell for her because it always does. Then, just after I told Martha too bad she couldn't sell hot date supplies at the movie high school, Starletta's teacher ran through the door and to the podium, disrupting the nurse's wrap-up to tell Ellen Foster to come down to go with her to the main hall immediately. Addled, she said it wasn't a general emergency, just Ellen's, and then she ran back to the door and waited for me.

I moved without asking why. The faster you go, the more likely they are to be alive. You don't need experience in getting there miraculously in time if you have new endings ready for everything you weren't able to run to before and so well-nursed and strengthened by the time they've spent in your heart that your movements can be swift and easy, recited like the gifts instinct offers at night, giving mendicant, palmer, pilgrim, prior, tricking and stopping, sleepy and proud, cried in goose, alas.

When I turned a corner onto the wide hall, I saw

people edged around the outskirts of a cyclone, yelling to egg Starletta on or to stop. Breaking in was like sticking an arm in a fan, and the adults who'd decided to wait on me to try it stepped aside and watched because they needed to send good will my way and flatter me into breaking up the brawl so Starletta's mother wouldn't have too many injured places to count and hold their noses to when Starletta got home. While they were shouting ways for me to stay safe and dodge flailing blows, I pushed through to the center and saw her arched in a flying leap onto a gigantic white boy's back. She held on and beat him with one hand, and then she'd clamp her legs and go at his head with both. When I found a way to get my hands to pull her off him, she was blowing like a horse and soaked from the milk from all the cartons scattered across the floor.

The boy was new but familiar to me because he'd frightened her before and caused her mother to come to school repeatedly, saying either they make him leave Starletta alone or she'd have to leave until they could tell her he'd been enrolled elsewhere. He'd loped out of the classroom behind her when she left to collect milk money from the grammar grade rooms and then waited for her to come out of the lunchroom, pushing a metal cart loaded with cartons. He knew her routine, how she stopped between rooms to handle the pumpkin pin and how she'd grip the bar and put her weight against it to keep it from drifting, overall getting the largest possible bang you could get out of a morning. When the boy couldn't take his craving for milk or beauty anymore, he'd lurched out to rob her the same way he had before. This time, she wouldn't turn loose of the cart, and so his last good time for a while was drinking the fourteenth container of milk she let him have in peace.

I carried her to the library and let her down onto the large satin pillows she's always luxuriating on in the Easy Reader section, blissful, but when I covered her with the sweater Mrs. Delacroix handed me, she turned on her side and stiffened with her hands pressed between her knees and her eyes closed. You could hear the commotion of the boy in the office, and Mrs. Delacroix said, Go to my desk and call her mother. I'll watch her. Hulking sonabitch, grain-fed fool.

Her mother wanted to know the details on the phone so she could begin sorting them on the way there and not appear, swinging. When she arrived, she was quiet but ruthless in a way she didn't care whether colored women had free permission to behave or not. After she was in the office a minute, she changed Starletta into a dry dress she'd come in holding and said, Go get her things. I'm stopping by Laura's for her to help me think, so come if you want to go home, but don't stop to linger.

Starletta's classmates scattered like shot pool balls after the brawl, so I was able to scrape out her toy- and candy-jammed cubby into my book satchel in peace and then rush to the library, where Mrs. Delacroix said Starletta's mother had been in a white woman hurry to leave and motioned to where they were waiting in the car. I flopped in beside Starletta, who lay her head in my lap while her mother drove, kneading her legs.

I said, How did you do it? If I'd been in your shoes, I would've gone blank and let him sit on the cart and offered him straws. To answer, she pulled up her dress to show me the two pairs of underwear that she wore on mornings when her mother showed her the calendar to remind her of milk days and other times when she knew the extra sensation of being held securely would help her stay brave.

Eleven

THE UNKNOWN CAR IN THE YARD DIDN'T GRAB MY
attention as much as Laura flying out of the house
like we were the rescue squad there to save her. Slowing
down as she came toward us, she was wild-eyed and staggering on the heels she disliked wearing on the thick
gravel. As we got out of the car, I said, You look like
Ava again, after she's been with her house boyfriends in
the ocean. Are you trying to keep us from seeing the
Spaniard who owns this car? I was wondering if this is
what you did with the day while I was in school.

She said, No, your aunt, your cousin, your lawyer
sent them over.

When Starletta wrapped herself around her mother's chest with the same stubborn grip she'd held on the boy, I said, She either senses what's in the house or remembers, and that's fair warning for me to get my bicycle out and ride her to the store. I know I said I wanted to talk to them, but she's in the flesh now, here.

Starletta's mother told Laura, I don't know if you notice it isn't time for school to turn out yet.

Laura looked down at the business-looking pumps she would've worn to a lawyer's office and asked herself why she'd worn them on sharp rocks. Then she said, To tell the truth, I wondered a second, and my mind turned it back, absolutely out of room after a world of information this morning and then these two inside. What's wrong? Starletta looks unstrung.

Starletta's mother said, I offered to bring Ellen home after she took Starletta away from a mess, but it can save for us to go on into this one.

Walking inside, I didn't see a box or bag in the living room, but Laura nodded and motioned to say my mother's belongings were outside in my aunt's car. It was fishy that it hadn't come in with them, so before they could stand up to greet me, I had to ask whether they'd left their car locked.

Aunt Nadine was still tight fat, like there was a hidden place on her where skin was stretched together and safety pinned, and I knew her tone would say I was still abnormal, but it didn't matter. She shimmied to the edge of the sofa and screamed, Well ho! Look who's here and not any more able to wait a minute, but you wouldn't think it, not with how grown you've grown, and in the paper all the time with the prizes and so forth and so on, like somebody else.

She meant it as a compare and contrast of the present me to the disaster ingrate she'd told to leave her life, with Dora agreeing, rabid to get rid of me and rip through the remainder of her many Christmas presents. There hadn't been much more room for Dora to continue into on the growth chart, but the baby on the way drove her over the highest percentiles. I said, Hey Dora, I'd like to run out there and get the box so you don't have to worry about accidentally taking it.

Dora said, I won't. I'm the one that packed Aunt Shine's things for you.

I sat by Laura on the ottoman she'd rolled in front of the fireplace, and as Starletta's mother came back in from settling Starletta to play in my room, I realized how Dora was the only person I didn't become highly jealous of when I heard her say my mother's name. So few people who said her name like they knew her deserved to, and when Dora said it again, I didn't hear myself shouting inside like a hateful toddler, Mine.

Dora said, I put so much in, I thought I better not try to come up these steps with it, but I'm glad to go with you to carry it.

And you know how my back is, my aunt said, nodding at me like her pet bodily complaint had been on my front burner.

I whispered to Laura, We're getting the hustle.

Laura said, And you couldn't begin to know. The box can't compare to what I need to talk to you about.

But Ellen needs to look at Dora first, my aunt said, and tell me if she doesn't look like something.

Laura said, She looks very nice, about to pop. I'm going to get the papers we're here to talk about and be right back.

Dora was mortified, and Starletta's mother and I were mortified for her, so critically that the least painful thing I could find to ask her was, Where did you find your bracelets?

Still looking down from when her mother had spoken, Dora said, I was about to ask you that about your top, but they come from somewhere in town I forgot.

We got them, her mother said, when we got the news and decided to spruce up because of how hard it is to stay girlie the heavier you get.

Starletta's mother got up, abandoning me to check on how quiet things were in my bedroom. She had to go back there and stand stunned that a woman who used an awful silliness to make her coarseness pleasing could've been related to my mother. I'd always believed my aunt genuinely loved her sister, but now you sensed somebody who wasn't graceful or smart, scratching to keep up with the older one who was. I saw it in how unsteady she was, how out of place she looked in our house. I wasn't as afraid of her, on my ground, in a room that Laura made, and with Laura coming back in now, with more of my mother's favor than I'd seen.

Sitting by me with a folder on her knees, Laura said, And you've considered flying to Texas, I'd think. It's a long way of open opportunity to be stranded, this far along.

When my aunt said the doctor outlawed flying, Dora said, What he said was don't go at all.

I'd never seen anything as dejecting as my cousin's permanent wave, which, she said, kinked on account of the hair chemicals either don't take or overtake when they mix with the pregnancy chemicals.

She kept looking down and peeking up, like she was checking to make sure we weren't glued to the other ways her mother had decorated her to appear old enough for a baby. Four years ago, we would've glared one another down, and now I tried to look only in her eyes or not toward her at all so she couldn't tell I'd noticed the round blue earbobs sized like vanilla wafers her mother had no doubt shoved her into buying to go with the wide bangle bracelets, a necklace of blue and white painted wooden beads, thick suntan hosiery off the spinning Queen Bee rack, not pretty improvements but mean ones, temporary, and in the main so out of season it broke your heart in a million pieces on the floor by her bad-looking, wee-heeled vinyl shoes.

It hadn't occurred to me until right then that people in the same family weren't automatically in the same category of basic life culture and taste. The comedies feature stories about the poor relations, and there's Daisy Miller not knowing how to act, but in thorough realism, every atom of my aunt was so distant from my mother,

I would've bet Harvard that the papers on Laura's knees had to do with the discovery that my mother had been adopted and her parents were alive very elegantly somewhere and wanting badly to meet me.

Laura tried to speak but my aunt couldn't let it happen yet, saying, Is that the same haircut you had before, Ellen?

You wouldn't hear it as a trap set by someone who wanted me to fear I was funny-looking, which I knew I wasn't, not because Stuart said I wasn't but because lately I was washing my hair. I looked up and said, Oh, I'm turning out in the face. Having a maldeformed feature or being overall, vaguely ugly was something I'd avoided, a large piece of good fortune and rare. So I happened to be feeling confident with the bone structure and clear skin genes my mother had passed to me when my aunt added how lucky Laura was that my modesty over the accumulating accomplishments meant she didn't have to find bigger and bigger bowls to whack around each time I had my hair cut. Then she said, Ellen's always run her part down the middle and wouldn't listen to what it looked like.

Laura said, Ellen's not here to be spoken to like this. I'd ask you to simply say what you mean to say, but I don't see that happening, so these papers can do the talking now.

While Laura opened the folder and leaned over to separate the papers into piles on the floor in front of us, and Starletta's mother mumbled about the gall it took to give a running commentary on somebody, like they were owned, I remembered how John and Yoko protesting in bed had set my aunt off nonstop to where she couldn't drive and see a person in wire-rimmed glasses without threatening to run them down with the car. She ridiculed intellectual ideas and curiosity and felt better when people and things around her were mediocre. If you held your head up around her, you risked being made to feel beaten down or smothered, so different from the way Laura stood laughing in my door, not long before, holding books that had just arrived for the next set of weekend classes, saying, Theory of the Leisure Class and Growing Up Absurd, that's definitely us!

Bending over with Laura as she arranged the papers, I said, I should've admitted this before, but I part my hair in the middle because people with just a few brains have to do that to keep their balance.

Sitting up, she said, Do what?

Aunt Nadine, I said, tell Laura how hippies like John Lennon have to do the same thing.

When my aunt said, Ellen, that was just a manner of speaking, not something I meant, Dora said, Yes it was and still is, far as I can tell.

Dora could tell the truth on her mother, you could tell by the way she'd lifted her eyes and looked forward, because she understood her mother's meanness wasn't the theme of this room.

Laura said, Thanks, and now Nadine, I don't know you, so I can't judge whether what you've done comes with any kind of pleasure, although I'd imagine it was worrying about everybody in this community finding out and the pain that would cause has a great deal to do with moving to Texas. At least, that's what the rumor mill's grinding out. But from what Ellen's lawyer told me this morning, another mill's been grinding, slowly as it always does and exceedingly small.

When I asked Laura what she meant, she said, Something I remember from school, I'll tell you later.

No, I said, I know it's a symbol, but what's it been grinding?

Laura said she'd thought she'd known where to start,

but things were sounding disorderly already, and Dora said directly to me, You know how so much bad happened to you, and some of it just happened and some of it people did? Well, you have things coming to you from then, have had things, and you could take and put a bucket for it to all grind into, I think is how she meant it.

My aunt began jabbing her eyes with a tissue, saying, Nobody's going to want to talk about how hard losing Shine was on me when everybody tries to make me out greedy.

Laura said, I'm willing to do that. We'll say you did what you did because of grief. I'll even ignore the fact that a grown woman losing a sister doesn't compare to Ellen going without her mother, and I won't mention how she's yet to develop any kind of mean-spirited plot or raged out at anybody because of it. She's been healing and going forward, and I don't see as you've stepped a foot out of the past. But I have to know this, before the lawyer brought your attention to it, did you think passing your daughter off as Ellen, introducing her to the president of a large bank, having her sign documents, did you think Ellen being there in the house and not able to save a woman determined to die from dying, did you think that entitled you to create a lie to take it all? Did you start talking about it on this road to try and get ahead of us finding out? I'd hate to have a daughter have to live with a mother who had to spend all the time and worry it must've taken to maintain the grip on that kind of hard knot.

Dora said, It kept her fairly occupied, and I said I may as well get something of my own going on, so I started dating some. But you know, I told her a thousand times I didn't want to go to jail, and she'd say I wouldn't on account of I was underage, and flip a quarter, and I'm headed to Texas, to the other side of the family I don't know anywhere well enough to walk in the door and have a baby with.

Laura said, I don't know why, but I assumed you'd be shy.

Probably, Dora said, on account of I hadn't talked to you before now.

And yes, Laura said, and so, where do you want to move?

I braced for her mother to shout rather than have Dora expose her desire to follow wither the circus band xylophone player who fathered her child went, but she excused herself to the bathroom, not to hear Dora say, This nice house on this nice street in Washington DC where this person just left to live and said I could come up there with the baby and see how it went. You have to be sixteen is the only thing hindering, and I turn that in two weeks, but Mama tries to say they don't make trains in Texas, like I'm going to follow behind her like a zombie and believe it, when she knows I used to only behave like I trusted her. Since I found out how she rooked Ellen, I can't act. But Ellen, don't think I'm trying to borrow from you because I may not be as set-set, but with what I have in mind to do, I and the baby are set.

Through the ringing that whined up in my ears, I heard my aunt in the back hall, inviting herself in to take a look at Starletta's playthings, making herself absent from the scene of Dora getting up to narrate through the papers Laura began showing me. Starletta's mother cried out laughing about how she was going to move onto our sofa bed and let our new uniform maid bring her sandwiches. I'll say, I don't want any of it, I'd like to enjoy being a little to the side of it, but I've got to find a cleaning replacement who loves bleaching grout as much as Ellen. This was quick. I expected a stream of ridiculousness before things came to what the matter is.

When I understood the matters well enough for the time, I told Laura I needed a minute off and asked to see who else was parched. She and Dora went to the kitchen, and Starletta's mother and I walked into my room and found Starletta coloring in the Mamie Eisenhower chair with my aunt, sitting on the arm, holding the box of crayons opened down for her and saying barely to be heard, You and I'll sharpen these before we're through. Then she looked at me and said no louder, I couldn't stand for you to accuse me now, so please, if you wouldn't. I didn't take, Ellen, but I know I kept and everything I kept would've been your mother's. I want her, and I despise it with her gone. I hated people to love her. She'd loved them back with what I needed, so when I saw a way to keep something of her, I did, but it's there now and yours. Nothing was wasted, the worth's become more, so maybe you can do what I couldn't and have it mean something to you. I can't see that anything matters without Shine. Do you see?

Oh, I see, I told her. I know about scrounging for something else to feel like it matters.

Going to pick up Starletta, her mother said, Excuse me, I understand why you kept all the money and land, but it was Ellen's by law, and you got caught and made to hand it over. You both know Shine would say she's still owed because you took so much other, and anybody with a soul and sense would say, Ellen, is there anything I can give you or do for you after all this, now?

Ellen knows I'd do anything, she said.

No, I don't, I told her. Nothing's expected from whom nothing was given.

Whew, it was time, Starletta's mother said, waiting for me to follow her back down the hall, for a fresh motto, healthy, wealthy, and wise.

It was also time for my cousin and me to have a way to say what was possible for us to have now between us. She made me let her carry the box to the steps, and after she set it down, she said, That's done. I'm glad, and Ellen, you may not remember, but I always enjoyed being around you and your mother. She was kind. Mine wouldn't be like she is if she could be different. Okay, well I need to get on. I'll see you again soon though. Don't you think?

Yes, I said, and it'll be something to look forward to next time, without all this other.

When I put my arms around her, I thought we'd mash in together, not realizing how hard an eight-month stomach is and not expecting the quick, rounded knot I felt traveling across my skin. A knee, she said, or foot. So, see you next time.

And until then, I told her, remember the Alamo and you'll be fine. How could you not be? Mother of God, you've actually got a being in there, waiting, Dora, playing around.

Twelve

WHEN MY AUNT AND COUSIN LEFT, STARLETTA'S mother lay down on the sofa and asked to hear the story in a sane, slow way now that Dora wasn't there to jump in to point out things she didn't want me to miss, like how much income the farmland around my parents' house had made each year. I was headed toward my room with Starletta and the box, but sent her on and listened. A lawyer had called Laura this morning, saying to come to his office so he could explain everything to her.

And the first thing the man said to you was what? Starletta's mother said.

Please don't get me disbarred, Laura said, smiling.

He'd grown up in town, an old family, another world, gone to Harvard, come home eager to please. Ellen's grandmother's estate was the first one of any size he handled alone, and even though he thought Nadine was a crackpot for not having her mother's lawyer handle it, things flowed, things were divided, Dora signed Ellen's name where she was told and didn't appear capable of much else besides nagging her mother. When Ellen wrote the letter to Harvard, to Dr. Bok, who ran the law school before he became president, Dr. Bok called asking if he'd heard of this local go-getter named Ellen Foster who's broke and wants to start college early. He said he'd read one of Ellen's columns she'd sent along with her letter, as well as her picture from when she won the speaking event in Washington. After he called the lawyer, he phoned up Nadine.

As I was sensing the wad of confusion Dr. Bok probably felt that told him the trouble I'd declared over was actually cranked open and definitely to be avoided, Starletta's mother said, Nadine could've gotten on with the Republicans to break into the Watergate.

I know, Laura said, it doesn't seem possible, but she blindsided the young man and rolled over him. He was still edgy this morning.

But did he phone up Harvard, I asked, and make things right or was he afraid of looking like a criminal fool?

Laura said, Oh, I'm sorry, I'd meant to say, yes, he did, and he needs to see us as soon as he can get your aunt's end of things straightened out. Needless to say, all the documents need to be redrawn, and some decisions have to be made about your aunt.

Let her go, Starletta's mother said. With the light on things here, this end is fine, and Texas is large enough to make her feel small as she needs to, and then she can be decent with the baby and allow her daughter to feel what it would've been like to have a human raise her.

When I said I hope things ended or began like that, Laura said, Don't you think it has to, with everything moving in a direction? We'll find something to lay out for supper if you want to take the box on to go through it.

An inventory among the papers had said everything else was in my grandmother's house, and the keys for that, my old house, and a dozen tenancies were with the lawyer now, so I could go anytime and take anything out and handle it. Even though what had been in our four rooms could've fit in the box if Dora had wedged things in right, what had been in my grandmother's house would've made a sizeable grocery store feel crammed, all the shelves filled with silver, crystal, tapestry, gold. Though part of me wanted to hog it, I saw my grandmother glaring over the plates we ate countless individual chickens or turkeys on, determined I was going to break one, determined she could will me not to. I didn't think I loved her, I liked her the way you do old ladies, hard-crazed by loss, who guard their magnificent stuff in a book, and before I closed my door with the box and Starletta resting on the bed now, I called down through the house, telling Laura, You could be serving supper on gold dishes here directly if you can carry me to the big house to get some of, well, my booty.

Starletta had fallen asleep in the middle of the opened carry-around town I kept in my closet for her to play with. In the category of the giant weatherman and car salesman, I think she believed it was the one from her house with the missing traffic cop and grocer somehow present, like they lived in my closet when she went away. It was so pleasant and truthful a thought of her gorgeous double-underweared self that it would've taken more than I had, in light of the day, not to lie down by her and haul heaving, weeping for everything I didn't have but I did now, saying it was certainly sufficient, fine, filled, enough, before I opened the box.

Dora had taken care to use blue tissue and leave the lightest things for last. Moving the paper aside, I saw a yellowed Western Union message addressed to my mother at Bay View Apartments in San Francisco. Thirty-two years before, he'd said the words aloud for someone to type, and he sounded kind when he'd spoken

My dear Shine. Stop. Meet me at base Sun. noon with clean civ shirt. Stop. Make res. at Cliff House our table. Stop. Hawaii a wonder but so is my darling wife. Stop. Your loving husband.

Starletta had opened her eyes and sat up as I was reading. I said, I'm sorry. You needed to rest. Your mother and Laura are cooking, and I know they're talking about what happened at school. We've had a red-letter day, evermore one, but Mother of God, Starletta, look at those.

I reached a double strand of pearls over her head and read a note from a report card underneath them, where the teacher wrote, Ellen knows what to do and does it, a joy to teach, and my mother's answer in a Palmer penmanship hand, Ellen is smart at home as well and I admire how hard she tries with her lessons. Can we please speak sometime on whether to be concerned about too many cartoons?

I found the gold compact wrapped inside an embroidered pillowcase, and after we'd opened and closed it a few times with it up to Starletta's ear for the snap, I gave it to her to handle and looked through tat-work aprons and antimacassars, the Girl Scout uniform from when I was living with my father and tried to be organized until it seemed too lonesome and embarrassing after a couple of weeks, a yellow cashmere sweater with hazy flowers my mother didn't wear because it was too nice, prickled through now with holes, and a red tin cash register I didn't remember. Dora had taped a note on the back,

Hey Ellen,
   You'll need one bigger than this one. Ha ha. But serious, beware not to flash what's in there in front of my mother or you'll draw back a nub. I'll send you where we are so you can tell me if you think Oscar and Maybelle sound like names for just dogs and help me think of names maybe out of

books as well as the best way to leave where I am, a funny feeling to have before you get to somewhere. Okay, just wanted to slip this in since I'm by myself for a minute. You won't believe it but best wishes always from your cousin.

The long October scarve I'd wanted was folded inside another layer of blue tissue, the last thing before some typed papers I set aside for Laura to put with the others. Unfurling it across the bed, I found a brass or gold lipstick holder, with a scene of a lady stepping up into a carriage circled around it, etched it felt. It was missing the tube of red with the white wax circle of what had tasted like a menthol medication when I took it out of her purse and put it on and when I used it, the last time, before we left the house for the funeral. Maybe it melted during a summer, while it was stored, I didn't know, but I couldn't let it stay empty or wait, so I tried the tube of coral Laura gave me. When it fit, Starletta sighed, relieved, and handed me the scarf, which I hadn't remembered being dark gold velvet on one side with the fall leaves against black silk on the other. I said aloud, But it is, and then wrapped it around the head that had dipped

down to smell and touch and sympathize, I believed, saying, She carpe diems extremely and it's fine.

While I was removing some rusted pins from the
padded tomato wrist cushion my mother wore when she
sewed, I asked Starletta if she thought it was right that
a bracelet that favored a Girl Scout craft project was
the height of flair for jewelry my mother felt was good
enough for her. When I said I hadn't known how little it
had taken to make my mother ashamed, I waited for her
to look at me with the intent to say maybe all the changes
would help give me the oomph I needed to begin remembering without always slipping under the surface and
reliving. I had to hear it from somebody, and she was
capable, although I mostly heard her through her eyes
that would open wide enough and fix on me as long as it
took to believe she'd just cored down into the truth. But
she was overly involved with pushing all the rings she'd
found in the cash register drawers onto her fingers,
thinking, I knew, that they were hers from the fair, not
knowing several were real and that the rest had come
from the Buster Brown chest at the shoe store.

She'd filled her fingers by scooping across the top of
the drawer, so three weighted, real rings were still there,

a gold band with a deep blue sapphire between two diamonds, a rectangular diamond on a gold band that I put on, remembering how it had looked too heavy for her, like something a businesswoman would wear. She'd worn the diamond with the plain, slim band I found, but they didn't amount to jewelry because even the mother of the family that ate off records wore an engagement diamond and wedding band. I put them in a box on my dresser, but I decided to wear the sapphire, telling Starletta, I think this is what I do now, you would, so there, and tell me if this doesn't look like a woman of means' hand now.

I picked up the folder and told her to come with me to leave it with the others and set the supper table. Halfway down the hall, she kept going but I called out I'd eat later and they'd understand a need for some time alone. Laura shouted over the loud frying, We know where you're coming from, just decided Starletta's going to stay home with her mother, no school, no big goon, not another minute alone, so have at it, sympathizing. You okay? Do I need to come see about something wrong with the box?

I said she didn't need to come and not to worry if she saw the door closed against the noise drifting back, just trying to be still on one of those days that called for it. When I opened the folder, I'd seen a date stamped in red beside the name and address of the state mental hospital, not a quiet, expensive one like Holden's parents would've put him in. We didn't have those, so poor or rich, you went to Dorothea Dix, a place named for a social crusader who would've shut it down if she'd been around to read the paper. If you'd read a story about the hospital, you wouldn't have needed the picture they always used of the high-spired, red brick building with the narrow, tall, barred windows to visualize what had to be happening inside, groaning, gnashing, bloodcurdling screams coming from people locked in and tormented out of their individualities and eventually released, after maddening years, into the world as zombies.

They were her admission papers, a kind of story to summarize her life and why her sister had brought her there. Looking at the date she entered and left, I couldn't remember a time when she'd been deadened in the spirit or walking dead, like the patients I'd imagined there. She was sad but there were things to be sad about, my father, her heart, the certainty that had set in with promises that nothing could change. And then the date, the tenth of September, six months before she died, said she'd missed

October, spent it inside, and what pity I felt for her family since my aunt left, was gone.

She was too modest to be grouped on a ward that I'd heard they organized by the county you hail from, not your ability to get along or illness. All I knew then about her as a girl was that she wouldn't allow the maid to collect her personal laundry, and she washed her things with chamomile soap, hung them on a rack she pulled a shy curtain around, and then pressed them before she laid them back in her dresser by lavender sachets. I remembered days when I got home from school and she wasn't there, when Starletta's mother would be there to walk me across the yard and explain how everything was fine, she'd gone to the doctor and he said she'd feel better after a few days in the hospital, that's all, and she would've packed a grocery sack with clothes to spend the night at her house.

These dates said she'd been away for five weeks, and thinking back through pictures of old afternoons, the sensation of falling into a particularly deep hole came back. The only means of climbing out was the voice I heard in the story I'd lay on my bed with, a woman talking to my mother with a patient kindness to let her know, to let me know now, everything was well. Hearing the woman, it wasn't surprising days afterward when I saw among other papers a bill marked paid by my grandmother for the private room with private bath and fenced terrace she'd arranged for my mother, who'd come for rest and had hell enough in her own room with her husband at home. Despite weeks of rest, time with her that felt stretched forward to infinite then I saw now as a timeline with the arrow replaced by an absolute stop. We'd gathered almost everything we were going to, and I hadn't known,

The patient presented as a frail, neatly dressed white female, with attractive regular features, and introduced herself simply as Shine. By turns despondent and hysterical throughout the interview, she was sometimes confused and delayed with her responses, but she was not delusional. Her chief complaints were fatigue and depression. She responded slowly and deliberately, frequently crying. She asked and was allowed to lie down and rest.

She was referred for evaluation by her primary care physician, who expressed concern—see attached document—that her general lethargy would postpone the open-heart surgery indicated by her last cardiac examination. He recommends that staff use the broadest possible admissions criteria—her spouse's inability to comprehend the critical nature of both her mental and physical condition is, in his opinion, endangering her life. During her absence from the home, he will continue his ongoing discussions with the husband about obtaining inpatient treatment for his alcoholism from the Veterans Administration.

The patient expressed severe anxieties about the impending heart surgery, though she denied her fears are in any way related to the fact that the procedure is innovative and invasive. She doubts her ability to survive her recovery. When questioned, she said she is terrified that when she visualizes her nine-year-old daughter playing in the yard next summer, she does not see herself sitting on the steps to their house, watching her.

She repeatedly said that if she could only get stronger, she could be there, but she feels herself getting increasingly weaker, with physical sensations of wasting away until nothing is left of her. The patient is convinced of her worthlessness as a parent and rebuked gentle suggestions that her views may be tainted by her current depression. She is afraid that she will soon be debilitated to the extent that she will not be able to care for her daughter, recounting detailed, imaginative fears of the child starving with a mother nearby but unable to prepare a nourishing meal.

She was brought to the hospital by her mother and sister. When told that the patient was being admitted to a ward rather than a private room, both women became combative and verbally abusive. They said the patient was from a quality family and threatened to file a complaint even after it was explained that her risk for suicide would increase if she were left alone. The patient asked them to be quiet or go home, at which time they left the patient's bags and departed, again threatening legal action if the hospital allowed other patients to steal or destroy their contents.

The patient calmed considerably. After standing to say good-bye to them, she asked to remain lying down during the remainder of the intake and frequently apologized for being exhausted. When told that her latest cardiac tests showed adequate justification for her complaint, she insisted it was her own fault. Nursing staff interrupted intake at 11:40 to record vitals, which were sent to the medical department for preparation of her chart.

The patient began asking repeatedly after the care of her daughter during her hospitalization and was reminded that the girl would be cared for by her sister. When she was offered assurance that her husband was at home for additional immediate support of the child and that her physician was seeing to her husband's own recovery, she became hysterical. She was administered .5 mg. Valium PO.

She responded to the proverbs as follows:

Spilt milk—Don't cry over things that aren't real.

Thrown stones and glass houses—Be more at home, and try to keep it neat. You should live in a brick house if possible. It can't come down. But why would I throw a stone in my house? I wouldn't do that. I didn't.

Wolves in sheep's clothing—You can't get help from the wolves if you don't have any power. You have to have money to have power. I used to be rich. If I were a wolf, I could get rid of him. It wouldn't matter what clothes I was wearing. My mother buys Liberty fabrics for my daughter's little dresses. Did I tell you that?

Rolling stone and moss—Don't be irresponsible. If
you're forced to roll, you could scrape off the moss.
Clean up the mess you made. I made a mess of my
life. Did I tell you that?

When asked about her home life, she said she wasn't
lonely, that her daughter frequently stays in bed with her,
coloring and playing school. When asked to describe a
recent occurrence that brought her pleasure, she said it
was watching Ed Sullivan with her daughter, who surprised
her by singing along all the words to a song. She became
distraught and could not continue. The interview was
halted while she rested and was administered oxygen,
after which she appeared more comfortable.

When further questioned about her family, she said
she worshipped her child but was terrified that life was
getting away from her. She said she'd made a deal with
the devil when she married her husband, who seemed
determined not to let either of them have a long and
happy life. When asked to explain, she said she married
him to get away from home and have the excitement her
parents had shielded her from, although she described her
adolescent years as lovely and very happy.

She said he was clever and good-looking, so she was incredulous that he was attracted to her. She described his family as being well-off enough but hard-living, and though she initially enjoyed the fact that he didn't treat her with kid gloves and didn't make concessions to her often delicate health, his coarse treatment of her escalated as her health declined.

The key events in her marriage were the birth of her child and the death of her husband's father, which occurred in the same year. She said her husband lost his way permanently at that time and began drinking continuously. Not only does he miss his father's direction, he misses the time he spent on an aircraft carrier in the Pacific, she said, and often seems to live in the past and regret that nothing as exciting has happened to him since.

She became inaudible, saying she had to admit something terrible and embarrassing. The night before, her husband had broken a lamp on top of the television because a program with the actor Robert Stack was on. She said he stays livid with the actor because they were on the same crew aboard the ship and the man has done considerably better. When asked if the child witnessed the violence and if she has ever witnessed such an outburst, the patient rolled over and faced the wall, saying nobody would believe it if they were told.

When asked if the child needed to be removed from the home before her mother and sister could collect her, she said her husband actually idolized the child in his own way and is counting on her to live out his old dream of an exciting life. She said he was too lazy to take advantage of the GI Bill yet sees himself as a neglected grand man.

She asked the staff's opinion on the question of what would happen to her daughter if something happened to her and then answered that people would know her husband was unfit and would remove her and raise her correctly. She says she will keep pressing her family for forgiveness for marrying someone they despised and putting herself in such a dangerous position and hopes they will, in turn, care for her child. Hysterical again, she said the child would suffer whether she lived or died, and she felt tortured by the embarrassment of having a child look up to a mother who wouldn't defend herself and let them live at the mercy of a cruel and negligent man.

Note that a message was forwarded to the North Ward desk at 12:10 recommending that her 15-minute suicide checks be elevated to constant watch for at least the next 72 hours.

She claimed no support from her husband and said he makes her afraid by overdrawing their accounts at the bank, and part of her feelings of worthlessness involve a dire sense of having deprived her daughter of things and said if the child didn't have the bookmobile and TV, she'd have nothing at all. She said her husband humiliates her by saying she lived well enough as a child to last all her life and seems unconcerned that the lack of air-conditioning and physical labor required in a rural home, for example, make her heart condition worse.

She produced five one-hundred-dollar bills from her dress pocket, saying her mother had given the money to her that morning and told her to use it for an escape, but she was too tired and asked the staff to keep it locked away from her husband should he arrive. Her mother, said she, put ten thousand dollars on deposit for the child's education when she was born, but her husband took the money and she is still too afraid to ask where it has gone.

When asked if she had ever considered divorce, she said she was too miserable and weak to go through it and would not know how to be a person without a home and a husband to care for. She claimed to love her husband, although her affect was flat when she spoke of him.

Her childhood background was marked by the onset of scarlet fever at five years old with a resultant rheumatic fever, which led to her coronary debilitation. Her father was her primary caregiver as her mother was too impatient. He named her Shine, she said, because she sang at the table. He gave her a new car for her last birthday at home and also for completing school with a perfect academic and attendance record. She said he set an example with his lovely manners, and then she said he died during her fourth year of marriage, at which time she asked for a cup of water.

She left a teachers college before the end of her first semester and moved to Alameda, California, and worked as a secretary at a shipyard while her husband was in the Pacific. She said they were married on the steps of a courthouse in San Francisco with many other couples. When asked if this was a pleasant time, she said she had a nice, neat kitchen and went out with other wives and listened to music, had tea at a nice hotel, and sunbathed on the cliffs sometimes but since arriving home twenty-five years ago, she hasn't really done anything social.

She says she enjoys her neighbors but can't have them in her home and going to theirs has become too sad. When her mother or sister take her for medical appointments, they take her shopping, although she has to remove tags so her husband will not cash in the purchases.

She was well-mannered at all times and brightened when describing her daughter as a kind and funny child who seems oddly precocious. Her daughter has been real rather than play help, she said. She learned to walk holding a broom.

Her weight, 98 pounds, was attributed to eating nothing but cookies and cakes when her child is in bed with her sometimes on days she can't get up, which are becoming more frequent, as are fainting spells and attacks of neuralgia.

When questioned about the two fainting spells her sister reported her as having in a single week she said she'd wanted to finish cooking without her daughter knowing so she could stay outdoors with a friend. Crying again, she asked that the staff not tell her child that she'd fainted and was an inadequate parent. She claimed to have several acquaintances who could come by and help, but she is ashamed to admit she needs help when she brought the problem on herself.

Her daughter, she said, gave her what she needed inside, although she said she didn't know what she would do if the fear and despair became larger than the love she felt for her child. She then became nonresponsive and moderately catatonic in affect.

She signed the documents with difficulty but legibly and was admitted for a recommended six-week course of treatment for major depression and anxiety. Before leaving the area, she asked when she would be allowed to rest again and expressed fear of being around loud and out-of-control people.

She was administered .25 mg. Navane BID and placed in a wheelchair. Her person and personal possessions were searched with staff present to witness.

Removed from her purse—One gold mirror compact—One nail clipper—Driver's license—Social Security card—child and patient's eye and dental appt. cards—One small glass frame—envelope addressed to patient containing twenty one-hundred-dollar bills, typewritten hotel reservation for mother and child, train confirmation to Warm Springs, instructions for leaving area upon discharge, letter of credit, from office of pres., Providential Bank—child's school picture removed and placed in her pocket with one red Chap Stick—Gold case removed. Money, Items to be secured. Will call sister re appt. cards—call bank re courier delivery of envelope contents.

Removed from her person—One bottle Digitalis, 100 mg./50 prescribed to patient—One bottle Valium, .5 mg./40 prescribed to patient's sister—One matchbox containing 20 ct. yellow pellets, assumed to be a household poison.

Listen to her, shivering desperate, with poison in her pocket and the means for us to go to a place that sounded comfortable, far, and serene.

It was dark outside now, and everything that had happened since the sun came up that morning accumulated and wouldn't be swallowed down, and though it was Monday, it felt like Sunday evening, too late to begin anything, too soon to end, willfully holding back hours from passing, frustrating you out of going and doing. I sat at my desk with the papers, thinking, Little wonder she killed herself between Sunday and Monday.

When I looked in my dresser mirror, I looked chaotic in the face. I'd forgotten how quickly order flies off the rail until Laura opened the door and I told her, It needs to stop being Sunday. You think I can afford to pay it to be gone? I swear before God, all I want to buy is a shearling coat and time.

She took the papers and looked through them, sighing and moving me with her, saying, The fireplace, we were throwing cloves on it to kill a burn smell. Sit by it and let me look at these, what, admission records?

Yes, I said, but the last page is it. It's it.

Folding a blanket narrowly away from the fire, she sat on the floor in front of Starletta and her mother arranged on the sofa, I told them, like a birthing. I didn't ask whether anybody realized how convenient it was that they were both available to shape themselves into a simile. I asked, Did anybody know my mother and had I the means to go to a place called Warm Springs? Can you see the connotations and all the routine chances we missed? And now I can get a charge out of knowing we almost made a narrow escape to somewhere that favored the atmosphere this room would have in it right now if I wasn't spending all the power of positive thinking here on not coming apart. And let me tell you about this other. You know how I enjoy irony? Well, I'm having some kind of time knowing I've been miserable since she died because she died so I wouldn't be miserable. She thought she was a failure to me because she couldn't go and do like most, and it was already almost more than you could bear if you woke up first and saw her. I didn't know she was going around needing her hands occupied to stop her from killing herself or I would've made sure they were taken, you know, all the time.

Starletta's mother turned on her side and said, You couldn't tell what was on her mind by any means you used to try. If she'd lived toward this house and Laura had known she was sad or tired, she would've been offered a bed of nice linens and tea on the tray, but nobody guessed how bad she felt and helpless to reverse it. If you'd known, you and she would be at the other end of the sofa with us.

Looking at Starletta's wrap head, I felt myself envy the way she knew what made her happy and did it regardless of the day or hour. She didn't stoop in the doors of little houses, examining, and she didn't have a catalog of poems on life passing her by or a state of panicked absence to crawl in when she missed her mother, she darted into rooms until she found her. I watched her while I listened to her mother say I was lucky to have money to throw at my problems. Although money hadn't solved the girlhood woes of her inspiration, Madame C. J. Walker, she'd built a mansion to live in while she was trying. The women, she said, who live on in time, lived inside their time and did with it. They didn't believe waiting pertained to them and wore the second set of pants when they had to.

She would've crawled in the fire if she believed it was necessary for Starletta to be happy, and I saw what my mother had done had nothing to do with anything but one woman's ability to believe deeply and allow passions, convictions, truth, nothing watered down, and to love so enormously that the space would naturally be as large. My mother's love was what I was made of, and I'd been filled already, never endured a time when I wasn't, but I didn't feel it until I understood that she intended to die, and she intended to feel her love present, not remembered like something missing that I had to stay scrambling to have back. Laura called me to come over to where she was on the floor and show her the ring, her arms and legs already opened, listening to me saying the ring had been hers, telling me, I know, I know, and I love you, I know.

Christmas Eve
1975

IF YOU LIVE IN A TEMPERATE CLIMATE, I HOPE YOU awaken to snow. If you live in a continuous frozen zone, I trust you're enjoying a sturdy igloo and kind people to share it with, and if you're in a tropical locale, I expect you've accumulated some imagination, and things such as spray snow for your Christmas tree and bulk cotton balls for tabletop displays of cheery scenes of winter.

No matter where you're living, I hope you sleep peacefully tonight and waken into relief, not so hounded by worry you miss listening for the reindeer feet, even if you've grown older, as I have, and depend on memories of thrilling wishes. With no regrets or grudges against the tin and timber real life around you, let it be time to bring every memory inside like wood you place in the fireplace piece by piece, wish by wish. The old need that wasn't met, the wants misunderstood, what you absolutely knew and guessed, what you dreamed or half invented, saw and heard outright or saw and heard in words you read and adored, what was done to you and calls for revenge you let burn away. Each thing is of the same good use, and burning together, continually, the light the bundle makes belongs to you, your love and work, what you see by, how you're seen. By December, I understood the deeper the dreams and beliefs, the brighter and warmer you and the rooms you walk through are, and you're safe now passing through old places, not dark now, more than sufficiently kept lit by you.

Late in the afternoon on Christmas Eve, I answered when Starletta's mother called just before we left for her house to be sure we weren't bringing anything besides, she said, the set of sheets you'll need to sleep on the sofa pulled out and scissors. Mine, I've yet to find from unpacking. Oh, and you know the low shoe shelf in your mother's closet that things like to roll across the slope of the floor and be under? Bringing tape would save me from having to get on my hands and knees with clean clothing on or sending Starletta in to investigate. Hold on for me to think, yes, we just needed a safety pin for something, the clasp on her Rudolph's broken.

When I said it sounded like they were making a Halloween costume, she said, It feels like ten years went through my body, and the mind's following.

I said, I know. I'm still sorry it wasn't as easy as it sounded to get you into my old house and my friend from his sinking one into yours. If it weren't for Stuart, we'd still be hauling the family of four's leavings hither and yon.

I've never seen anybody as proud as he was to offer a pile of burning rubber to us, she said. He rode by yesterday and fixed a cold window for me, where the new seal fell out, and Martha rode by this morning with several very pretty things for Starletta, saying she's able to watch her for the classes I need at night now, and then days through the summer. So when you're around, you and she can take her to the city pool, movies, and so forth.

I know, I said, and Luther talked to Martha's mother and got on at the store. When I met him in the pasture this morning to trade gifts, he asked if taxidermy work qualified him for a promotion behind the meat counter.

She said, Where I got these livers I'm doing my thing

with here, and Starletta's doing her thing, plugging in lights, cracking nuts, what have you. Is your mother about ready? Oh, but tell her I don't need her old fireplace screen. After the masons finished, they accidentally hid the screen and poker setup behind Shine's garden shelter for Starletta to find and turn into a playhouse.

You know, I said, I could get the veteran to build her something like Mrs. Tom Thumb lives in at the fair. A miniature house has her number all over it. When we get there, I'll wrap one of the houses from her carry-around town, and don't say it's too much or coming from not having a place to bake mud when I was little. I'd do it for the charge of watching her set up housekeeping.

Laura had come in to stand, listening, and then she took the phone and said, The landlady and I will be over there directly. If I were you and trying to study and keep Starletta occupied, I'd be mixing concrete instead of batter. Remember the day you pulled her out of school, when you came over for us to think and then had so much other happen? Well, regard it like Ellen's making good on the ideas I've owed you and see if that takes the edge off getting a present on Christmas.

As Laura and I came around a curve and saw the bridge, where the road straightens toward what everyone was easily calling Starletta and her mother's new house, we slowed to see how much closer Marvin's old house was to floating off and agreed with others who'd begun slowing or stopping on the bridge for the same reason, thinking, Whew, just in time. Even though Marvin and his father were going to be cooking something they'd shot and opening gifts they'd carved by the tree they'd cut down and still so choked up by their new home they probably wouldn't be able to make a great deal of sense talking, we turned down Starletta's old path with their gifts, an electric shaver chosen for the father because he needed one and a pop-up toaster for Marvin, for how staggered he'd been the morning he came to pick up the house keys from us and learned Pop-Tarts were invented to be eaten hot.

They weren't at home, and no dogs barked, so I left the things on the steps for them to find when they returned from hunting and told Laura, They can snack and groom before supper at least, let's roll on.

The family of four was confused and unwilling to ignore the infinite lease my aunt had given them so she could think less and less about the house and what happened there, but they dashed with little more than the clothes on their backs when the lawyer made them the offer I said they couldn't refuse on account it involved moving to the verge of town, where houses start being closer together in rows. Laura and I knew they'd be ambitious for one of the split-level rentals on the scraped orange clay lots.

Their house looked beaten down in a hot hurry though, which said they'd settled in well and were living out their human nature, dirtier but no different at heart from what Marvin and his father, Starletta and her mother, and Laura and I were trying to do. Organizing them out of my old house was important to help keep chaos down after decisions exploded toward us, although the action cooled as my aunt and cousin straightened their end out in Texas and began doting on the baby, a girl, seven pounds, named Claire Ellen.

When Laura called to make our first appointment, the lawyer told her things didn't get this unfamiliar and he'd meet with us at home as much as possible. He came that afternoon, and as we watched him going through his satchel on the hood of his car, a diesel, Laura said, He's young but if I could start over at twenty or so, I'd go for that, expensive, studious, rangy-boned.

Narrow-assted, I said, is what Faulkner would call his shape in the hips. And now's not the time to ask and you don't need to tell me, but why didn't you get married?

Because, she said, the subject never came up.

I said okay then and let the man in. After we got through the whipping he gave himself for goofing so severely, he said, Before we go forward, Dr. Bok sent a letter and asked that I give it to you and explain that the help he refers to is mine, not that I wouldn't offer it or need another job if this estate doesn't get me fired.

I don't know, Laura said, as this estate goof-up is my kind of comedy. Though I can certainly see the potential, I think Ellen's earned the right to tell it like it's funny first. Don't you think?

Oh, I said, taking the letter, unless this is Dr. Bok saying after he heard about the ordeal with my aunt, he gave my spot to Walter Mitty because he already had all the female sociopaths he could use.

While I was reading the letter, Laura took him in the kitchen, and over the sounds of her making coffee, I heard, If Ellen can't find a word for something, good or bad, it's floored her. You'll be working with her, so you should know, she's not making herself up for your benefit. I could shake her in the middle of the night and ask her what Jack the Ripper was, and she'd say, murderer, sociopath.

I heard him say, I saw a copy of the letter she sent to Harvard and wondered, as you would, about things at home, especially with the serious size of this estate she's inherited and you, as the guardian and trustee, in the most influential position to guide things. But what you just said, is that fairly typical conversation around the house?

When Laura told him she supposed people bloomed where they were planted and he didn't answer, she said, The library in there isn't wallpaper, and if it was, Ellen could've searched sample patterns and talked to me about sociopaths simultaneously. She's happiest doing both and requires it. Her having a dollar in one part of her life and a million or more in the rest doesn't concern me. What does though is how quiet she is with the letter. It'd help if I knew.

When I was through, I took the letter to her, saying, You don't need to strong-arm him, Laura, here,

Dear Ellen,

I've asked my friend to give you this note, along with the enclosed information about Harvard we've gathered for you. He is looking forward to helping you to continue your extraordinary achievements. He was an excellent and memorable student, and although I have doubted that his hometown would offer him enough challenge and room to grow, I am confident you will provide him with both.

I've taken the liberty of meeting with my colleagues here who are in charge of our admissions procedures and requirements. After reading your letter and reviewing your application and supplementary documents, we all agreed that you are Harvard material and then some. We want you to know that your place in the Class of 1981 is guaranteed. However, we want you to flourish here, and we do not believe that beginning a conventional undergraduate program at fifteen is the best means to that end.

We propose that you begin attending summer classes this year, residing in one of our women's dormitories. We hope you'll want to return for each of the following two summers before you graduate high school, and, perhaps after your se-

nior year in high school, enroll in one of our over-
seas summer programs. The summer courses you
take will accrue credits that will count toward grad-
uation requirements when you enroll as a full-time
student in the fall of 1977. I'm confident Harvard
will be as enriched by your presence as you will be
stimulated, as you so thoughtfully expressed, by the
intellectual environment.

At Harvard, we're proud of our tradition of
educating those most worthy, and while I am extremely pleased to hear your financial circumstances have greatly improved, we want to offer
you a full scholarship. During your college years,
you should not feel compelled to apply yourself to
any endeavor other than expanding the already
considerable scope of your mind and building your
character, which is clearly unusually strong.

All the information you need to apply to this
summer's program is enclosed. Please do not hesi-
tate to call our admissions director with any questions that arise. I hope you will let me know the
date of your arrival this summer. We'll leave the
books behind and go on, I suppose you would say,

a walking, talking tour along the river. Until then, Miss Foster, congratulations on all you've accomplished, and I greatly look forward to meeting you this summer.

Your friend,

Derek C. Bok

I told Laura, I bet I can do this, don't you think?

Saying, Think it, know it, you're here, so yes, Laura answered the same question each time we waited outside the door to my mother's old house. Stuart had reinstalled the doorknob, but I wasn't able to turn it and walk nonchalantly through yet, like the place hadn't mattered. I was still studying neglect on Christmas Eve, while we leaned against the door, holding presents and knocking with a toe. When we heard Starletta running from the front of the house, I told Laura I'd be interested to know why I felt better inside the house than waiting.

Mother of God, she shouted, Starletta's coming toward us with new blinking shoes. We can sort through leftover nerves, Ellen. Watch her, just watch that, regard her high-voltage feet!

As her mother held back the door, she said, Santa Claus decided to bring the shoes early. We needed something to set the right tone, but, Ellen, I want you to feel free to think about not spending the night. It's Starletta's long toes under her foot lights, and it's Shine's house inside all the Christmas we put around. This may not be the time yet.

I told her and Laura, Being here, if you stand right here, and just be standing, you don't have the sensation of the floorboards opening up, and I don't think the ground's going to come up at midnight and swallow the bed, but I could use another October. Maybe not. One more of those may be called for.

What I believe, Laura said, is you knowing the time's coming will work well for you, Ellen, knowing it's certain.

Being obligated to carry change and lean every element toward winter, October couldn't keep the sky waiting. It had to come before the leaves could be released, like a permission. October's slightest responsibility still had the universe hinged on it, various safeties regarding the wind and extremes of temperature that could freeze a continent or sink it. When you compare and contrast the duties you stay expected to perform because of all the outlandish gifts you were given when you were little and talents you were furnished in your womb, if you accumulated everything that's ever expected of you, they'd never amount to more than the kind of mean little pile of coins misers sit around and trick between their fingers continually, not much of a wonder of achievement at all.

It wasn't an accomplishment either, realizing I was less important than the weather, it was a red-letter event in the history of an older girl looking toward the rest of the changes due to come on like seasons, rowed like the houses along my road, turning over like plowed ground folding. That kind of occurrence would automatically have something to do with love. Laura gave me love, but my mother's spirit was the light I needed to show the way into her, and she was able to stop straining to reach me. We rested from the giving and taking and stayed still together, telling one another we could do this through any commotion, going and doing and doing it well. Knowing well that I could be more than what my mother did, more than the moment she died—I am what she was before and is now, here with me in the burden of her love I'm content to carry, gorgeous to me and lighter than breath.

11/09-13